There's an Angel on Your Shoulder:

Angel Encounters in Everyday Life

THERE'S AN ANGEL ON YOUR SHOULDER:

Angel Encounters in Everyday Life

Kelsey Tyler

BERKLEY BOOKS, NEW YORK

THERE'S AN ANGEL ON YOUR SHOULDER

A Berkley Book / published by arrangement with
the author

PRINTING HISTORY
Berkley trade paperback edition / May 1994

ISBN: 0-425-14369-4

BERKLEY®
Berkley Books are published by The Berkley Publishing Group,
200 Madison Avenue, New York, New York 10016.
BERKLEY and the "B" design
are trademarks belonging to the Berkley Publishing Corporation.

PRINTED IN THE UNITED STATES OF AMERICA

10   9   8   7   6   5   4   3   2

Acknowledgments

This book would not have been possible without the numerous people who contributed their stories to my effort. I wish to thank each of them and assure them that a purpose has been served in making these stories public. Thanks to Maria Amato for uprooting herself and taking special care of my children during those intense writing times. You are the best, Moe!

I want to thank my husband for encouraging me to turn my dreams into realities, and my children for showing me a little bit of Heaven every day. Also, thanks go to my parents, who continue to be my primary source of feedback, and to my forever friends—Susan Kane, Pat Winning, Jo Ann, and Amber—who heard this book before I put it into print and who believed, as I did, that every one of these angel encounters was possible. I sure miss you all!

This book is dedicated to
the family of Christian believers
around the world,
especially those of you who
have truly helped me in
my walk of faith.

And to our Savior and Lord,
Jesus Christ

May we all be encouraged
daily by His
guiding hands and
mysterious ways,
even perhaps by His
angels.

A Note to the Reader

Are not all angels ministering spirits sent to serve those who
will inherit salvation?

Hebrews 1:14

Several years ago I came across my first angel encounter. I was a
new Christian at the time and was attending a camp at Angeles Crest,
outside of Los Angeles, when I heard counselor Chris Smith tell an
impressive story. For months afterward, I found myself sharing his
story with other people, always amazed at the details.

After that I began to wonder. Was it possible that God really used
angels to minister to those who believe in Him? In time, I began to
hear more such stories. I started putting together a collection of angel
encounters so that those who also had such experiences would know
they were not alone; and so those of us who had not would be
comforted by God's amazing presence around us, perhaps looking
more closely the next time a stranger helps us on some deserted desert
highway.

In putting this collection together, I had the privilege of talking
to most of the people whose encounters are detailed in this book. In
some instances, the people involved requested that they be referred
to by pseudonyms to protect their privacy, and this has been done.
On the few occasions when it was impossible to contact the people
involved, the details were provided by someone who heard the story
first-hand and believed it to be both truthful and completely credible.
In these cases, names are fictitious and are not intended to represent

specific living persons. However, it is not the intention of this book to prove the validity of these angel encounters. Instead, they have been written for your pleasure, to evaluate and take at face value.

It is my prayer that you, the reader, will gain from these stories a deeper assurance of your personal faith and a comfort in knowing that God is near. Sometimes closer than you might ever imagine.

Preface

Do not forget to entertain strangers, for by doing so some have
entertained angels without knowing it.

Hebrews 13:2

Why is mankind fascinated by angels? Songs sing about their presence, films bring to life their existence, and through the ages people
have speculated about their possibility. When we put faith in scripture,
as millions of people have done throughout the ages, we must at some
point address the question of angels. If these heavenly messengers of
God appeared to common people in biblical times, why would they
not also appear today to those who believe they exist?

Science, for all its technological wisdom, has never proven the
existence of angels. Perhaps the closest we will come to knowing
the truth about angels is in sharing the fascinating and unexplain-
able angel encounters of others. For a time, angel encounters were
described as sightings of winged beings, oftentimes robed in white or
ethereal coverings. But in modern times, stories of such sightings have
become more specific; the angels, more humanlike, their tasks, more
immediate. These encounters tend to have in common mysterious
people who perform a rescue or relay a message and then suddenly
disappear without explanation. Often, people who have had such
experiences will seek out the person who helped them, only to find
that he or she never existed.

For instance, the time a woman sat crying and praying at the
hospital bedside of her terminally ill husband and was comforted

only when a male nurse entered the room and offered to sit with her. For more than an hour he comforted the woman, assuring her that her husband was going to be all right in the place he was going. The next morning, after her husband died, the woman asked about the male nurse, wanting to thank him for the comfort he had brought in those final hours. "Ma'am," she was told at the hospital desk, "we have no male nurses on staff."

The following pages contain a collection of these lifelike angel encounters, relayed in detail as accurately as possible. A few of the stories have become modern-day folklore, told time and again around the world. For these stories, much of the detail is not verifiable and can be taken only at face value as handed down from one person to the next.

Others, though, are entirely documented, complete with times, dates, names, and eyewitnesses. There is a remarkable similarity between these stories and those that cannot be documented. We are left to wonder whether the stranger who disappeared without an explanation might have, in fact, been an angel.

Miracle on
the Mountain

hris Smith had driven the road a hundred times. He had spent the past seven years as full-time counselor for Angeles Crest Christian Camp, a retreatlike cluster of cabins nestled 7,300 feet above sea level, atop the San Gabriel Mountains outside of Los Angeles. The winding, dangerous road was part of the life he and his family had chosen.

Since taking the job and moving to their mountaintop home, Chris, twenty-eight, and his wife, Michele, had watched their family grow. Their oldest child, Keagan, was now nearly five, Kailey was three, and Michele was five-months pregnant with their third child. Chris and Michele loved the thought of raising a large family in their mountain cabin and couldn't have been happier.

Chris, blond with blue eyes and the good looks of a suntanned surfer, had no regrets about choosing such a secluded lifestyle for his family. With crime and over-crowding pressures in the city, their little mountain cab-in suited him perfectly. He enjoyed the thrill of watching busloads of hassled people arrive at the camp each week and leave days later renewed in their faith and attitude. When work was over and Chris headed back toward the cabin, he and Michele would take the children for hikes to explore the wilderness around their home. Theirs was a rewarding life and one that he and his family had come to cherish.

On the warm summer afternoon of August 10, 1991, Chris finished organizing the details for the next group of campers and walked through tall pine trees to his cabin, adjacent to the main hall.

Michele's face lit up as he opened the door and entered the room. He smiled at her, amazed that she seemed to grow more beautiful each day.

"Finished?" she asked as he pulled her into a hug.

"For now. The campers will be here this evening."

It was 2:30 p.m. and there were still several hours before darkness would blanket the mountain. For a moment, Chris and Michele remained in an embrace enjoying the solitude and closeness of each other. But suddenly a door opened near the back of the house and their two children came running into the main room.

"Daddy! Daddy!" Both children squealed with delight and raced toward Chris, jumping into his arms. "Play with us, come on, Daddy! Let's play tackle!"

Chris laughed. Keagan and Kailey were the joy of his life. The two blond children were full of energy and laughter and enjoyed nothing more than spending time rolling on the floor with their father. Chris could hardly wait until the new baby could join them in this ritual of afternoon play.

For thirty minutes Chris played with the children, laughing and tickling them until, finally, they lay stretched across the floor exhausted. Michele, entered from the back of the cabin where she had been busy working in the kitchen, into the main room, humming to herself.

whispered the words, his head hung in quiet desperation. "Now please, please let me find Kailey."

He stood up. "Kailey!" he yelled as loudly as he could, his voice choked by sobs. "If you can hear me, I'm coming to find you, sweetheart. Can you hear me, baby?"

Chris looked straight up at the rocky mountainside he would have to climb to reach the road. Suddenly, he saw people standing along the road's edge waving toward him. Then he remembered the cars that had been following him so closely. Someone must have seen the accident.

"Are you OK?" a man yelled, his voice echoing down the rocky canyon. Nearby, another passerby was already using a cellular telephone to call for help.

Fresh tears flooded his eyes as he screamed back, "Yes! But I can't find my daughter!"

Moving as quickly as possible, Chris began making his way up the hillside toward the people. He had begun coughing up blood, and his head felt as if it were about to explode. Still he continued to call Kailey's name every few feet. Finally, when he was forty feet from the road, he heard her.

"Daddy, Daddy," she cried. "I'm here!"

Chris felt a surge of hope and refused to give in to his body's desire to pass out. He had to reach her. "Kailey, I'm coming!" he shouted.

At that moment someone standing alongside the road pointed downward. "There she is!" Suddenly three of the bystanders were scrambling down the cliff toward a small clearing hidden from the road. They reached the child at about the same time Chris did. Kailey was sitting cross-legged on top of a soft, fern-fronded bush. Her eyes were black and blue, and she had dark purple bruises around her neck. She was shaking and crying hysterically. Instantly, Chris thought her neck must have been broken.

"Be careful of her neck," he shouted. "Let's lift her together."

"Yes," someone shouted from a few feet above the place where Kailey was sitting. "Let's get her up to the road."

Chris managed to stand beneath two men, helping to push his daughter up with his remaining strength as the others hoisted her to the highway. At about that time a medical helicopter landed on the highway twenty-five feet from the spot where Chris's truck had tumbled over the cliff. Paramedics began running toward Chris and Kailey, surrounding them and swiftly administering emergency aid. Within minutes, father and daughter were strapped to straight boards and air-lifted to Huntington Memorial Hospital in Pasadena.

Chris's head had swollen to nearly twice its normal size from the number of times it had slammed into the back of the truck. His lungs were also badly damaged from the pressure of his seat belt, which definitely saved his life. He was placed in intensive care and given a slim chance of survival.

Meanwhile, Kailey was taken to the pediatric unit where she was held for observation. Doctors took X-rays and determined that despite her severely bruised neck there was no damage to her spinal column. She had no internal injuries and had even escaped a concussion. Several hours passed before Michele got word of the accident and was able to rush to the hospital.

When she reached his side, Chris was unconscious, hooked up to numerous tubes and wires. His head was so swollen and his face so badly bruised that she hardly recognized him. She held his hand, crying and praying intently that he would survive. Then she went to find Kailey.

The little girl began crying when Michele hurried in, muffling a gasp at the sight of her bruised neck and eyes. Michele sat beside her quivering child and took her shivering body into her arms.

"It's OK, honey, everything's going to be all right," Michele mur-

mured as she tried desperately to appear strong. "Why don't you tell me what happened?"

"Oh, Mommy," she cried harder, burying her head in her mother's embrace. After several seconds, Kailey finally looked up, tears streaming down her face and began to talk.

"We were driving and then we started to fall," she said, her eyes brimming with fresh tears. "Then the angels took me out and set me down on the bushes. But Daddy kept on rolling and rolling and rolling." Kailey began to cry harder. "I was so worried about him, I didn't know if he was ever going to stop rolling. Is he OK, Mommy?"

"He's going to be OK," Michele said, but she was trying to understand what Kailey had just said. "Sweetheart, tell me about the angels."

"They were nice. They took me out and set me on a soft bush."

Michele lay her daughter down gently on the pillow and ran her fingers over the purple bruises that circled her neck. Suddenly a chill ran the length of her spine and goose bumps popped up on her arms and legs. Angels? Taking Kailey from the car? She remembered scriptures that spoke about angels watching over those who love God.

"Do you know my angels, Mommy?" Kailey asked, no longer crying, her honest eyes filled with sincerity.

Michele shook her head. "No, Kailey, but I'm sure they did a good job getting you out of the truck. Sometimes God sends angels to take care of us."

Over the next few days, as Chris's condition began to miraculously improve, sheriff's investigations learned more about the accident. First, they determined that no one had ever survived a fall of 500 feet along the Angeles Crest Highway. Typically, even if a person is wearing a seat belt, the head injuries caused by rolling so many times cause fatal hemorrhaging.

Second, they found the Ranger's back window completely intact and only a few yards from the highway. Although they had never seen this happen before, the window had popped out in one piece upon initial impact with the steep embankment.

Next, they determined that Kailey would have had to fall out of the tumbling truck on the first roll for her to have landed where she did. Which meant that in a matter of seconds the back window must have popped out and Kailey must have somehow slipped through the straps of her seat belt and fallen backwards through the opening onto the soft bush.

"A virtual impossibility," the investigators later said. In addition, the area was covered with sharp, pointed yucca plants. Had she landed on one of them, the wide shoots that jut out from the plant could easily have punctured her small body and killed her. The soft bush where she was discovered was the only one of its kind in the immediate area.

"From all that we know about this accident," the investigators said later, "we will never know how Kailey Smith survived."

For Kailey, the explanation was obvious.

Months later, after Chris had made an astonishingly quick recovery and was home helping Michele with their newborn son and busy preparing the cabin for Christmas, Kailey continued to speak matter-of-factly of the angels who pulled her from Daddy's car, set her on the soft bush, and kept her safe until Daddy could reach her.

Left with no other explanation, Chris and Michele believe their daughter is telling the truth about what happened that August afternoon. About her very special encounter with angels.

Modern-Day Prodigal Son

rom the high station in life he has attained, Charles A. Galloway, Jr., can scarcely remember the rebellious teenager he was more than fifty years ago. Back then, in the winter of 1938, he had done things his way, regardless of his parents' deep concern for his life and future. During that time, an event took place that would change Charles's life forever.

The son of two loving and devoted parents, Charles had grown up in Jackson, Mississippi, and had been privileged with a wonderful childhood. But during his teenage years he had grown restless, anxious to experience a wilder lifestyle. At age sixteen he decided he no longer wanted to stay in school.

"Charles, I absolutely will not hear of you dropping out of school, you hear me?" his mother said when he presented her with the idea.

"But Mom, I wanna be a prizefighter! I can do it, Mom. Give me a chance!"

"Nonsense," she said, turning away and shaking

her head in disgust. "No son of mine is going to leave school for prizefighting."

His father agreed. "Stay in school, son. You don't have a choice."

The relationship with his parents became more and more strained. Charles waited until school was out for summer vacation and made plans to run away from home.

"I just need to be a man," he told one of his friends before he left. "Gotta set out on my own."

Charles was an intelligent boy, tall and athletic and with an innate sense of survival. Because he had only a few dollars, he knew he would first need to find work. After only one afternoon on his own, he discovered that by watching the railroad cars, he could determine approximately where they were headed.

He watched the station for nearly an hour. As with all train stops, this one was protected by railroad bulls, large club-bearing guards who kept people from stowing aboard the boxcars. When the trains began moving, the railroad bulls would climb aboard and ride near the front of the train. They were not worried about people stowing aboard while the train was moving, since to do so would have been foolishly dangerous. For that reason, it was rarely attempted.

Charles could imagine the dangers associated with jumping onto a moving train, but he was not afraid. He determined he would wait until the train was moving and take his chances. If his timing was right, he believed he could run alongside a slow moving train and jump aboard one of the cargo cars without incident.

Summoning his courage, Charles waited for a train which appeared to be heading north out of Jackson and then made his move. If he missed, Charles knew he risked falling under the train's wheels. He forced himself to think positively, and at just the right moment, he jumped, landing safely inside the boxcar.

"Easier than it looks," Charles muttered confidently to himself.

He used his new mode of transportation several times over the next few days until he got off the train in a small Missouri town and saw what appeared to be a traveling carnival set up under a large banner that read "Red-Top Circus." His money spent, Charles approached the circus officials and was immediately hired as a roustabout.

"I'd also like to do a little fighting, if you don't mind," Charles added cockily, sticking out his chest as if to demonstrate his worthiness as a fighter.

The circus leader looked him over skeptically.

"We'll see, son," he said. "We just might be able to use you."

Now that he had found a place to stay and a way to make money, Charles wrote to his parents. They opened the letter together, tears of concern in their eyes.

"I can't tell you where I am, but I'm safe," he wrote in that first letter. "I may even get to do some prizefighting."

Over the next eight months, Charles traveled with the Red-Top Circus to dozens of towns from Missouri to Nebraska. Eventually, the circus leader allowed him to participate in the pit fights, in which two men were placed in a sunken pit and allowed to fight until one dropped from the punishing blows or from exhaustion. Charles didn't lose a single fight. Each time he won, he would go back to his sleeping quarters, pull out some paper and write a letter to his parents.

"I think you'd be proud of me," he would write. "Sure, I'm not in school. But I'm living out my dreams. Please don't worry about me."

Meanwhile, Charles's parents were naturally very worried about their son. They had always provided such a steady environment for him and now he was a drifter, a roustabout and occasional fighter for a traveling circus. They handled their fears about his safety and his salvation by praying for him daily.

"Lord, please protect our son," they would pray aloud. "Keep him safe and bring him home."

In February, after a cold Nebraska winter took its toll on carnival attendance, the Red-Top Circus folded. Charles had enough money to take care of himself for quite some time. But he wanted to return to the south and knew his money would not pay for train fare. Resorting to his former method of travel, he stowed away on a series of trains until two weeks later he was in Hayti, Missouri. After a large lunch at a local diner, he considered his options. Returning home would be admitting failure. He really wanted to find another circus, somewhere he could resume fighting. That afternoon Charles scouted the area only to discover that the nearest traveling circus was about twenty miles south. He knew just the train to take him south, and he hid himself near the railroad station's warehouse, under the loading dock. There he waited for the perfect moment. As he crouched in the shadows, he noticed that the train, which was still being loaded, would be pulled by two locomotives. That meant the train would pick up a great deal of speed much more quickly than usual. It might even be traveling close to full speed as it left the station. But he had jumped on fast-moving trains before and was not afraid.

When the time was right, he ran toward the boxcar and jogged alongside it. Suddenly, the ground beneath him narrowed and he was running alongside a steep ravine. A few feet ahead he could see that there was no land at all alongside the tracks—only a steep drop-off. Charles knew he had just one chance. Jumping before he had picked up the proper speed, he thrust himself upward and landed partially in the open boxcar. But with nothing to hold onto, his body began sliding out. As Charles struggled to pull himself inside the car, he could feel the train gaining full speed. Terrified at his predicament, he looked over his shoulder. The train was winding along the top of a very steep and narrow canyon ridge. If he slipped out he would either fall beneath the train's wheels or plummet down the steep canyon to his death. He closed his eyes and tried to will himself into the boxcar. Instead, he could feel himself slipping.

"Please, God!" he cried out, his eyes squeezed shut. "Don't let me die here." But Charles knew there was no way to survive the situation; he was seconds from certain death.

At that instant he opened his eyes. In front of him stood a fantastic-looking muscular black man in his thirties. The man was staring at him intently but said nothing; he only reached down and pulled the boy by his arms into the speeding boxcar. Charles lay facedown on the floor of the car for several seconds trying to catch his breath and regain his strength. When he looked up to thank the man, he had vanished. The boxcar was completely empty. One of the two side doors was closed, as it had been since the train began moving. He glanced outside and shuddered. There was no way the man could have jumped from the train and survived. He had simply disappeared from sight. Charles sat down slowly in a corner of the car and began shivering.

Suddenly he knew with great certainty that he needed to get home. He stayed on the train until it reached Jackson and immediately returned to his parents' home. He told them about the man on the boxcar.

"An angel, son," his father said, as his mother took them both in her arms. "God was watching out for you," she said. "See, he brought you home to us."

Charles nodded. "Things are going to be different now. You watch."

Charles returned to school that week and a few months later, his faith renewed, was baptized in the local river. After graduating, he moved to Southern California where he spent two years working as a professional prizefighter before being drafted. Charles served in World War II with the 339th Bomb Squadron in the 96th Bomb Group of the Eighth Air Force. He flew twenty-eight combat missions over Germany, and in May 1945, he returned to Jackson and went into the construction business with his father. Working together, their business became both lucrative and well-respected.

Now, at age seventy-one, Charles shares his story with anyone whose faith needs reaffirming. He is convinced that God saved his life by sending a guardian angel to get his attention.

"My entire life would be different if it weren't for that single afternoon," says Charles, whose faith and love for God is always evident these days. "God used that angel not only to save my life but to change it into something that could glorify him forever."

A Stranger of Light in the Cancer Ward

he bad news came January 6, 1981.

Until then, Melissa and Chris Deal were by most standards one of the happiest couples anywhere. They were in their early twenties, lived in Nashville, Tennessee, and shared a passion for country music and the outdoors. They were constantly finding new ways to enjoy each other's company, whether by mountain-biking, hiking, or playing tennis together. Attractive and athletic, Melissa and Chris seemed to live a charmed life in which everything went their way.

That was before Chris got sick. At first the couple believed he was only suffering from a severe cold. Then they wondered if perhaps he had contracted mononucleosis. But the doctors chose to run blood tests; and finally, on that cold January day, Chris's condition was diagnosed as acute lymphatic leukemia. At age 28, Chris was suffering with the deadliest form of childhood cancer.

During the next three months, Chris's cancer slipped

into remission and he stayed the picture of health. Muscular at six feet two inches and two hundred pounds, Chris looked more like a professional athlete than a man suffering from leukemia. During that time, Chris continued to work and neither he nor Melissa spent much time talking about his illness.

At the end of that period, doctors discovered that Chris's brother was a perfect match for a bone marrow transplant. But before the operation could be scheduled, Chris's remission ended dramatically and he became very ill.

"I'm afraid he's too weak to undergo a transplant," Chris's doctor explained as the couple sat in his office one afternoon. "The cancer has become very aggressive."

The doctor recommended that Chris be admitted to Houston's cancer hospital, M.D. Anderson, for continuous treatment in hopes of forcing the disease into remission. Within a week, Chris and Melissa had taken medical leaves of absence from their jobs and both moved into the Houston hospital. The nurses generously set up a cot for Melissa so that she could stay beside Chris, encouraging him and furnishing him strength during his intensive chemotherapy and radiation treatments.

Living in a cancer ward was very depressing for the Deals, who had previously seen very little of death and dying. The couple talked often about how their lives had become little more than a nightmare in which Chris fought for his life amidst other people like him, people with no real chance of overcoming their cancer. Chris began to spend a great deal of time in prayer, asking God to take care of Melissa no matter what happened to him. He prayed for remission, but also asked God for the strength to accept his death if his time had come to die.

Months passed and doctors began to doubt whether Chris's cancer would ever be in remission again. By Christmas, 1981, Chris weighed only one hundred pounds. His eyes were sunken into his skull, and he had lost nearly all of his strength. He was no longer able to walk and only rarely found the energy needed to sit up in bed. Doctors told Melissa that there was nothing more they could do.

"I don't think he has much longer, Melissa," one doctor said. "I want you to be ready."

Melissa nodded, tears streaming down her cheeks. She felt completely alone and wondered how their happy life together had turned so tragic. She began to fear that Chris would die while she slept, and for that reason she dozed for only an hour or so at a time, waking quickly each time Chris moved or tried to speak.

On January 4, Melissa fell into a deeper sleep than usual and was awakened at 3 a.m. by a nurse.

"Mrs. Deal," the nurse said, her voice urgent, "wake up! Your husband has gone."

Thinking that her husband had died in his sleep, Melissa sat straight up, afraid of what she might see. But Chris's hospital bed was empty.

"He's gone! Where is he, what happened? Where did you take him?" she asked frantically.

"We haven't moved him, ma'am," the nurse said quickly. "He must have gotten up and walked somewhere. We came in to check his vital signs and he was gone."

Melissa shook her head, willing herself to think clearly. "He can't walk. You know that." She was frustrated and her voice rose a level.

Even if her husband had found the strength to get out of bed and shuffle into the hallway, he would have been seen. Chris's room was on the circular eleventh floor of the cancer hospital, and the nurses' station was a round island in the center of the floor. There was no way Chris could have gotten up and walked out of his room without someone spotting him. Especially since each of his arms was attached to intravenous tubing.

The nurse appeared flustered and shaken, and suddenly Melissa jumped to her feet and ran from the room. As she ran toward the elevators, Melissa's eyes caught a slight movement in the eleventh-floor chapel. Heading for the door and peering inside, Melissa was stunned by what she saw.

Inside the chapel, with his back to the door, Chris was sitting casually in one of the pews and talking with a man. He was unfettered by intravenous tubing, and although still very thin, he appeared to be almost healthy.

Melissa was filled with anger. Why had Chris left without saying anything? And who was this man? Melissa knew she had never seen him before, and he wasn't dressed like a doctor. Where had he come from at three in the morning? Melissa stared through the window trying to make sense of what was happening.

After several minutes passed, Melissa walked into the chapel toward her husband. At the same time, the stranger looked down at the floor, almost as if he did not want Melissa to see his face. She noted that he was dressed in a red-checked flannel work shirt, blue jeans, and a brand new pair of lace-up work boots. His white hair was cut short to his head, and his skin was so white it appeared transparent. Melissa turned toward Chris, still keeping one eye on the man across from him.

"Chris?" she said, questioningly. "Are you all right? Where have you been?"

"Melissa, it's OK," Chris said, laughing casually and appearing stronger than he had in months. "I'll be back in the room in a little while."

At that instant, she turned toward the stranger and he looked up at her. Melissa was struck by the brilliance of his clear blue eyes.

Who was he, she wondered. How was he able to make Chris laugh and appear so at ease when only hours earlier he had been barely able to move? Melissa stared at the man, mesmerized by the look in his eyes and searching for an explanation as to his existence.

"What's going on?" she asked, turning back toward her husband.

"Melissa, please, I'll be back in the room soon!" Chris's voice was gentle but adamant. Melissa knew that he wanted her to leave them alone.

Reluctantly, Melissa turned to go, making her way back to the center station where she informed Chris's nurses that he was in the chapel. They were relieved and did not attempt to bring him back to his room.

For thirty minutes, Melissa waited alone in the hospital room until finally Chris joined her. Melissa almost didn't recognize him. With a wide grin on his face and a twinkle in his eyes, Chris appeared to be full of energy as he walked toward her with a strength he hadn't had before. He was obviously happy and at peace with himself.

"OK, I want to know who that man was. Why were you talking to him? What did he say? And how come you're walking so well? What happened?" Melissa fired the questions at her husband in succession and he began laughing.

"Melissa, he was an angel."

His happiness and the way Chris spoke those words left no doubt in Melissa's mind that he believed what he had said was the truth. She was silent a moment, allowing herself to ponder the possibility that the man had indeed been an angel.

"I believe you," she said softly, reaching toward her husband and taking his hand in hers. "Tell me about it."

Chris told her that he had been jerked awake and instantly experienced an overpowering urge to go to the chapel. His tubing had already been removed, something none of the nurses remembered doing when they were asked later. As he moved to climb out of bed and begin walking, he was suddenly able to do so without any of his usual weakness. When he got to the chapel, he quietly moved into a pew and kneeled to pray. He was praying silently when he heard a voice.

"Are you Chris Deal?" the voice asked gently.

"Yes," Chris answered, curiously unafraid of the voice.

At that instant, he turned around and the man was there, dressed in a flannel shirt and jeans. The man sat directly across from Chris, their knees almost touching. For a moment the man said nothing. When he spoke, Chris had the feeling he already knew the man.

"Do you need forgiveness for anything?" the man asked.

Chris hung his head, his eyes welling up with tears. For years he had held bitter and resentful feelings toward a relative he'd known most of his life. He had always known it was wrong to harbor such hatred, but he had never asked for forgiveness. Slowly, Chris looked up and nodded, explaining the situation to the man.

The man told Chris that God had forgiven him. "What else is bothering you?"

"Melissa. My wife," Chris said, the concern showing on his face. "I'm worried about her. What's going to happen to her?"

The man smiled peacefully. "She will be fine."

The man knelt alongside Chris, and for the next twenty minutes the two men prayed together. Finally, the man turned toward Chris and smiled.

"Your prayers have been answered, Chris. You can go now."

Chris thanked the man, and although nothing had been said he somehow was certain the man was an angel.

"And then I came back here," Chris said cheerfully.

Suddenly Melissa leapt to her feet. "I have to find him," she said as she left the room.

Melissa believed Chris's story but she was overwhelmed with the need to talk to the man herself. She ran back to the chapel but the man was gone. Next, she checked the guards who were at their post at each elevator. She described the man Chris had talked with.

"A man in a flannel shirt and jeans," the guard repeated curiously. "No, haven't seen anyone like that."

Melissa hurried into the elevator and traveled to the first floor. The guards at the hospital's main entrance had also not seen anyone who fit the man's description.

"But that's impossible," Melissa insisted. "I know he had to have gone through these doors less than fifteen minutes ago. He couldn't have just disappeared."

"Sorry, ma'am," the guard said. "I haven't seen anyone like that all night."

Feeling defeated, Melissa returned to Chris's hospital room where he was sitting, his arms crossed in front of him, with a knowing look on his face.

"Didn't find him, right?" Chris said, grinning.

"Where did he go? I really want to talk to him." Melissa was frustrated, baffled by the man's sudden disappearance.

"I guess he went to wherever he came from, honey. He did what he came to do and he left."

Slowly, Melissa nodded as if she understood. She still wished she had been able to find the man, but apparently Chris was right. The man had completely disappeared, perhaps to return to wherever he had come from.

The next day when Chris awoke, even more energetic than he had been the night before, both Melissa and Chris thought he was miraculously in remission. He was happy and content and spent much of the day visiting the other patients on the floor and offering them encouragement by praying with them or merely listening to them. Many physical manifestations of his illness seemed to have lessened or disappeared as mysteriously as the man who had visited him.

Then, two days later Melissa awoke to find Chris staring at her strangely.

Suddenly nervous, Melissa sat up in bed. "What?" she asked.

"I dreamed about Bill last night," Chris said, clearly confused by the dream. "You told me to tell you if I ever dreamed about Bill."

Bill, Chris's best friend, had died in a car accident the year before. For reasons that were unclear to her, Melissa believed that if Chris ever dreamed about Bill, it meant Chris's death was imminent. She hadn't told Chris these thoughts but had asked him to tell her if he ever dreamed about Bill.

Now Melissa was confused. Chris couldn't be near death. He looked vibrant and strong. And if his prayers had been answered, as the flannel-shirted man had told him, then he must have been on his way to recovery. Something wasn't making sense.

"What about the angel?" she asked Chris, her voice filled with anxiety.

Chris shrugged. "I don't know. You just asked me to tell you if I ever dreamed about Bill." Something in Chris's face told Melissa he knew why she had considered the dream significant.

That afternoon, Chris suffered a pulmonary hemorrhage. He began bleeding from his mouth and nose, and immediately there were dozens of doctors and medical experts swarming around, desperately trying to save his life. Melissa moved to a place behind Chris's head and placed her hands on his shoulders.

"Come on, Chris," she shouted frantically. "Stay with me!" At that moment one of the doctors asked her to step aside so they could work on him.

Melissa backed up slowly and found a spot in the room against the wall where she sank down to the floor and buried her head in her hands.

While the doctors hurried about Chris, shouting "Code Blue" and trying to save his life, she began to pray. Almost instantly, she felt a peace wash over her and realized that this was part of God's plan. Chris had prayed that she would be all right, and at that instant she knew she would be, no matter what happened.

That afternoon, minutes before he was pronounced dead, exactly one year after being diagnosed with cancer, Chris called out Melissa's name.

"It's OK, honey," she whispered, her tear-covered face gazing upward. "It's OK."

Now, more than ten years later, Melissa believes that Chris's prayers had indeed been answered that night when he was visited by the man she believes was an angel. Since his time on earth was running short, he had been given the gift of peace, of accepting his fate and not fighting it in fear. Also, he had been released from the bondage of bitterness and hatred and graced with the gift of God's forgiveness. That fact was evident in the happiness and contentment of his final days. And finally, Melissa had survived Chris's death and came out stronger for the ordeal—another answer to Chris's prayer.

Although there are people who might try to explain or argue about the identity of Chris's visitor that night, Melissa saw him, looked him in the eyes and watched the transformation his visit made in Chris's life. As far as she's concerned, there will never be any explanation other than the one Chris gave her that same night: "Melissa, he was an angel."

Priority Check

oAnne Davis had never been one to put stock in material wealth. Even when she strayed from her religious roots as a young, independent college student, she cared little about the brand of clothes she wore or the make of car she drove.

Instead of things, people were the focus of JoAnne's life. When those around her were hurting, she felt their pain. When they needed a hand up or a handout, she provided it whenever possible.

When JoAnne turned thirty-two in the spring of 1993, through a series of unexpected circumstances, JoAnne wound up the owner of a brand-new yellow Cadillac sedan. By then she had found her way through prayer back to a strong relationship with God and believed that the car was a gift from Him. God had trusted her with such a car, she figured, because she did not hold great admiration for luxury items—thus, it would not interfere with her life in any way.

Still, the car was far different from the old practical

vehicles she had driven in the past, and she enjoyed being able to take friends places in style. She was not surprised that she was enjoying the car. What surprised her was the way in which God chose to test her priorities not long after she received the Cadillac.

It was a particularly warm day in June, and JoAnne had picked up her friend B.B. for a trip to the local shopping mall. The women were chatting casually when, just before they pulled into the mall's parking lot JoAnne spied a man limping along the sidewalk. He seemed to be in his 60s and he wore black slacks, a dress shirt and a tie—all of them tattered and torn. As JoAnne drove past him, she saw that sweat was pouring down his face as he struggled to move forward.

Then she glanced down and saw the reason for his struggle. Although he walked without the aid of a cane, the man's right foot was deformed, turning in severely at the ankle and forcing the man to bear weight on the ankle bone with each step.

"I can't believe that," JoAnne gasped, instantly aching for the man.

B.B. turned to see what had caught her friend's attention and sized up the man's situation. "How sad," she said.

Caught in the flow of traffic, JoAnne turned right into the parking lot, drove up one aisle and down another, parked her new car, and turned off the engine. From her vantage point, she could see that the man was still making painstaking progress along the sidewalk and suddenly she could no longer stand to watch.

"That's it," she said, starting the engine up once again.

"What?" B.B. asked, her hand on the door handle.

"I can't stand it. That man's suffering," JoAnne explained, pulling the car back into the aisle. She headed for the same area where she had entered the mall moments earlier. The man reached the spot just as she did, and JoAnne leaned out of her car window.

"Sir, can I give you a ride somewhere?" she said, loud enough that the man looked up and smiled at her.

"Why, that would be very kind of you," he said. "I missed my bus and I need to get back to my apartment. It's only a mile from here."

Ignoring the traffic that had begun to build up behind her, JoAnne climbed out of her car, opened her back door, and helped the man inside. Now that he was so close, JoAnne was nearly overcome by the stench from the man's filthy clothes. She glanced at the backseat of her new car. But almost at the same time she reminded herself that she had done nothing to earn the car. It had been a gift from God, in her opinion, and if she could use it to help a struggling human being, she would do so gladly.

As she got back into the driver's seat and pulled out onto the road, she asked the man exactly where he needed to go. Glancing in the rearview mirror, she noticed his strange hair color. For his age, the man's strawberry blond hair seemed unnatural. Also, he seemed utterly peaceful and unaffected by his condition. Whereas before he had been struggling so intensely, now he seemed rested and without a care.

JoAnne wrinkled her eyebrows in curiosity and struck up a conversation with the man. She talked about how she and her friend were going to attend a church program that night and how the choir had been working on it for weeks. When the man remained silent, JoAnne tried another approach to get him talking.

"Do you know the Lord?" she asked simply.

The man looked up suddenly and then seemed almost flustered. "Oh, well, that's another matter," he said quickly and then immediately pointed up the street at the apartment building where he wanted to be dropped off.

JoAnne considered his answer and thought there was practically nothing she could say in response. She cast a questioning glance toward B.B. who, also puzzled by the man's words, shrugged her shoulders.

"Here," he said, breaking the silence. "Right here. Thank you so much." He waited until JoAnne had pulled up to the curb, and then he began to open the door. She quickly got out and helped him up onto the curb. Then she took a piece of paper from her purse and scribbled her phone number.

"Here," she said, handing the paper to the elderly man. "If you ever need a ride or anything at all, please give me a call. I'd like to help."

As the man took the paper, he looked intently at JoAnne and smiled. "God bless you," he said softly. Then he backed up a few steps and watched as JoAnne returned to her car and prepared to leave.

But just as she was about to pull away from the curb, JoAnne suddenly wondered if the man did indeed live in the apartments. After all, he was still standing with his back to the entrance. Perhaps he was homeless and didn't have any place to go. Although troubled by these thoughts, JoAnne pulled back into traffic and began driving.

After passing two other buildings, she stopped abruptly and turned the car back to the apartment where she had dropped off the man. She had to know if he really had a home or if now he would be all alone again.

But as soon as she made the turn, she peered toward the sidewalk where the man had been standing seconds earlier and realized that he had vanished. She sped up and pulled up against the curb once more. The apartment entrance consisted of a long corridor with no doors opening off of it. JoAnne stared up the corridor but there was no one in sight.

"Where is he?" B.B. exclaimed, astonished that the man had disappeared.

"I don't know, but come on," JoAnne climbed out of the car and began trotting toward the building. "He's got to be here somewhere."

For ten minutes the friends searched the perimeter of the building, the bushes that ran along the front of it and up and down the street. The man was nowhere to be found.

Finally, they gave up and returned to JoAnne's car. They sat in the car and discussed the impossibility of what had happened. They had seen how slowly the man walked. His handicap would have prevented him from walking more than ten or fifteen feet in the time it took JoAnne to turn around and come back.

Suddenly, B.B. gasped. "JoAnne! What if the man was an angel?"

JoAnne leaned back against her seat and stared ahead pensively. She had always tried to help people in the past, had hurt for them sometimes more than they hurt for themselves. But then she had received the Cadillac.

"You mean like a test or something?" she asked, turning toward her friend.

B.B. nodded. "Would you still be willing to help people even if it meant opening your new car to a smelly, dirty, dejected man like him."

JoAnne thought a moment and then smiled. "There's really no other explanation, is there?"

"Not really."

"I guess I never thought God's angels looked like *that*," JoAnne said. "But it makes sense. Especially if it's a test of some kind."

"Well, if it was a test I'd say you passed with flying colors. What is it the Bible says about angels and being kind to them?"

JoAnne glanced around one last time and then started the car. She smiled and turned to her friend. "Be careful to entertain strangers. For in doing so, some have entertained angels without knowing it."

The Littlest Angel

 ouglas Tanner was exhausted. After fifteen years of neurological work in Boston, he had developed an extensive list of patients and an equally impressive reputation. But Tanner paid the price for his success, especially on days like this.

The hospital had been overcrowded, probably because of the cold, wintery weather that January 1957, and the accompanying increase in illnesses. In addition to helping tend to the swarms of people who seemed to line the halls of every floor of the hospital, Tanner had been busier than usual, with exceptionally burdensome work: several examinations and two tiring surgeries.

Tanner peeled off his navy cardigan sweater and shuffled into the kitchen where his wife, Cheri, sat at their kitchen table reading a women's magazine.

"Long day?" she asked with a gentle smile, rising to receive his embrace.

"Hmmm." Tanner needed no words for moments

like this. Cheri had been a part of his life since his days in medical school, and she knew by the look on his face what type of day he'd had. He sat down slowly, stretching out his legs and enjoying the sensation of muscles relaxing throughout his body. At forty-two years old, he was in very good shape and usually looked ten years younger. Today he looked his age and more.

"Dinner's in the refrigerator," Cheri said, tilting her head and waiting for his response.

"Maybe later. Right now I only need you and this wonderful old chair."

Suddenly, they heard someone run up their front steps and ring the doorbell. Tanner and his wife exchanged a puzzled look. It was nearly nine o'clock, bitterly cold, and snow had been piling up outside for the past two hours.

Tanner stood up and released a long sigh. "Who in the world could that be at this hour?" He headed toward the front room.

"Yes?" he said as he opened the door.

There, shivering on their doorstep, stood a little girl dressed in torn rags, a tattered coat, and worn-out shoes. Tanner guessed she couldn't have been more than five years old. She was crying and she turned her huge brown eyes up toward Tanner's.

"Sir, my mother is dying," she said, her voice choked by the sobs. Tanner felt his entire insides melting with concern for the child. She had the sweetest, purest voice he'd ever heard. "Please could you come? We don't live far."

Tanner did not hesitate. He turned quickly back toward Cheri, who waited behind him. "Get my sweater and overcoat, dear. I'll be back soon as I can."

Cheri smiled as she retrieved the items and watched her husband bundle up. Her husband had chosen the medical field because he enjoyed helping people. Now, with someone's life in jeopardy, he would not remember how tired he had been until he was home and the woman safely cared for.

Tanner took the little girl's hand and the two headed out the door and into the storm. Less than two city blocks away, in a section of tenement apartments, the little girl turned into a doorway and led Tanner up two flights of stairs.

"She's in there," the little girl said, pointing toward a bedroom at the end of a narrow hallway.

Tanner moved quickly toward the bedroom and found a woman who was very sick, fever racking her thin body. She was nearly delirious, her eyes closed as she writhed under the blankets, moaning unintelligibly. Tanner determined immediately that she was suffering from pneumonia and that he would need to bring her fever down if there was any chance to save her life. For more than an hour he worked over the woman, soothing her hot, dry skin with compresses and arranging for her to be transported to the nearest medical facility.

Finally, when her fever began to subside, the woman opened her eyes slowly, blinking because of the bright light. She saw the doctor, still working tirelessly to cool her body with wet rags, and she thanked him for coming.

"How did you ever find me?" she asked shyly. "I have been sick for so long. I might have died without your help. How can I ever thank you?"

Tanner smiled. "Your little girl saved your life. I would never have known you were up here otherwise. Thank her. Sweet little child, braving a cold, stormy night like this and walking the streets until she found me. She must have been awfully worried about you."

A look of pain and shock filled the woman's eyes. "What are you talking about?" she asked, her voice dropping to little more than a baffled whisper.

Tanner was puzzled. "Your little girl," he repeated. "She came and got me. That's how I found you here."

The woman began shaking her head and her hand flew to her mouth as if she were trying to stop herself from screaming out loud.

"What is it, what's wrong?" Tanner took the woman's hand in his and tried to soothe her sudden panic. "Your little girl's all right."

"Sir . . . " Tears were streaming down the woman's face as she was finally able to drum up the strength to speak. "My little girl died a month ago. She was sick for weeks and . . ." She paused a moment, bending her head and allowing the sobs to come.

Tanner stepped back, shocked by the woman's story. "But she knocked on my door and led me here! I held her hand until she showed me where you were."

The woman's tears were coming harder now and she pointed toward a closet in her cramped bedroom. "There," she said between sobs. "That's where I keep her things since she died."

Tanner walked slowly toward the closet, almost aware of what he might see before he actually saw it. He opened the door gingerly and there they were. The coat worn by the little girl only an hour earlier hung completely dry in the closet. The girl's tattered shoes sat neatly on the floor of the closet.

"These belonged to your daughter?" he asked, turning toward the woman.

"Yes, sir," she said, wiping her wet cheeks with the sleeve from her nightgown.

Tanner turned back toward the tiny coat and shoes. "The girl who led me here wore this coat and those shoes," he said, almost as if he were talking to himself.

Suddenly he turned and ran toward the room where he had last seen the little girl. When he could not find her, he hurried throughout the apartment from one room to the next. The little girl had disappeared. After he had finished his search he returned to the girl's mother.

"She's gone," he said flatly.

The woman nodded and suddenly her face broke into a smile, the tears replaced by a strange peaceful look. "Her angel has come back to help me. How else do you explain this?"

Tanner shook his head slowly. He had no answers for the woman. He walked home slowly that night, pondering the impossible and wondering about life. He had been gifted with the knowledge of medicine, a knowledge that often meant the difference between life and death in a patient. Yet, there was so much he did not know, so much he would never understand in this life.

Years later, he would tell the story about the littlest child who, although dead more than a month, had somehow summoned him from his home to help her dying mother. And he would still feel the same sense of amazement he had that cold, wintery evening. Although there was no earthly explanation for what had happened that night in Boston, he believed in his heart that the woman had been right. The girl must have been an angel. The littlest one of all.

An Angelic Reminder

hen her mother presented her with the idea. Amber Cook was anything but excited.

"Texas!" the nineteen-year-old minister's daughter shouted in exasperation. She had grown up in Southern California and enjoyed the beaches and sunshine and city atmosphere where she lived in Fullerton. "I hate Texas. There's no way I'm going to Texas."

The plan, her mother explained, was for Amber to meet up with one of their church friends in Texas where she would join an eight-member Christian singing group called Departure, which would travel the country visiting churches for one year.

"It'll be good for you, Amber," her mother said confidently. "I want you to at least think about it. You know you've been looking for a way to get out of town for a while."

A beautiful blonde with brown eyes and a singing voice that easily rivaled any of the professional recording artists, Amber was currently having trouble getting a former boyfriend to stop calling. Because of that, when Amber's mother heard about the offer, she thought the trip would give Amber the desired separation from the young man.

Amber shuddered at the thought of spending a year in small towns across the country. She had lived in Southern California since junior high and knew how much she would miss her friends. But Amber also loved to sing. She had dazzled local audiences since she was four years old and had occasionally been approached by talent agents. She had even developed a fanlike following among the large congregation where her father was minister. Someday, Amber always told herself, she would pursue a professional singing career. And though she was not quite ready to make that career move, the idea of singing nearly every night for a year was enticing. Finally, her desire to share her faith through song became stronger than her dislike for small towns. She agreed to fly to Texas and spend a week with Frank and Ruth, her mother's friends from church, and the other members of Departure.

At week's end, despite the lack of city luxuries, Amber was hooked. She flew home, spent a week packing and bidding her family and friends farewell, and then flew to meet the group in Baton Rouge, Louisiana. The group traveled from one city to the next in Frank and Ruth's motor home. Each night they would sing at a different church, hoping to soften the hearts of those in attendance. Typically, when the performance was over, they would collect small donations that would pay their food and gasoline costs until they reached their next destination.

For the first few weeks, Amber experienced an indescribable joy when she sang about Jesus to a churchful of people. There were many ways to tell a person about God's love, and her way was song. She felt as if God had a purpose for her life, and she could hardly wait for the concerts each night.

But as time passed, the joy of singing began to wear thin in light of the group's circumstances. Amber suddenly found herself focusing instead on the inconvenience of sharing a motor home with seven other people. There were occasional tire blowouts and breakdowns and times when the group's funds ran so low, there was no telling where their next meal would come from. In addition, Frank had a heart that was, in Amber's opinion, far too generous. If a needy person crossed their path, Frank would use their dinner money to buy him or her a sandwich, always believing easily that God would somehow provide their means. Even though they had never gone without, Amber was still bothered by Frank's total selflessness.

One afternoon, three months into the tour, the group stopped at a small southern seaside town for an Italian dinner. Weeks had passed since they had eaten anything other than fast food, but the previous night's offering had brought in enough that Frank decided they could afford a sit-down dinner.

As the group approached the restaurant, they noticed a man dressed in tattered rags with dirt covering his face and matted hair.

"Bum!" Amber whispered to herself in disgust. "Watch Frank invite him to dinner."

As the group drew closer to the man, Amber was horrified when Frank stopped and started up a conversation with him. Amber got closer so she could hear what they were saying, and suddenly she was assaulted by the man's body odor and the smell of musty alcohol on his breath. Stepping away, Amber guessed that months had passed since the man's last bath. Disgusting, she thought to herself. The man has no pride in himself whatsoever!

Through their conversation, Frank learned that the man was homeless. He had been on the streets for the past year and needed some money for food. Frank smiled. There was only one way to be certain the man used the money for food.

"I can't give you any money," he said gently. "But we'd love to have you eat dinner with us. Our treat."

The homeless man looked skeptical. "You wanna bring me the food out here?" he asked, refusing to believe that Frank might actually want such a man eating with his group.

"No, of course not!" Frank said, waving toward the restaurant door, where the manager was watching them in conversation. "Come in! Eat with us."

The man stared at the members of the group, his eyes resting on Amber. Then he shrugged and stood up.

"What's your name?" Frank asked as they moved inside.

"Gus."

Amber dropped toward the back of the group and rolled her eyes in frustration. Now they'd have to smell this filthy man for the next hour and no one would enjoy the meal. She shook her head and followed the others into the restaurant. The tour really wasn't working out like she'd hoped.

Once inside, the manager showed them to a table near the back of a large, square-shaped room. Amber sat down first and waited for the others to fill in beside her. When everyone had found a seat Amber was horrified to see that the seat beside her was still empty. The homeless man still stood off to the side, unsure of whether he should really join the group at a formal dinner table. He looked embarrassed as he scanned his ragged and torn clothing.

"I'll just go outside and wait," he said suddenly. "You can bring me something out there if you want."

Frank stood up and shook his head. "Absolutely not," he said, pointing to the seat beside Amber. "Sit right there."

Amber slid as far away from the empty seat as she could and prayed she wouldn't lose her appetite. She already felt suffocated by the man's putrid smell.

Just ignore him, she told herself, determined to enjoy her meal despite the man's presence.

After the group placed their order, the man looked at Frank and began to speak.

"Where are you people from?" he asked, making eye contact around the table.

Frank cleared his voice. "We're just a traveling Christian singing group. Call ourselves Departure," he told the man. Amber pretended to be studying her silverware. If they were really a traveling singing group they would certainly have a more luxurious set of circumstances than these, she told herself wryly.

"Christians, huh?" Gus asked doubtfully. "Well, Christians, I have a few questions for you." The man waited until everyone, even Amber, was watching him attentively. "You people are always talking about how much God loves me. How am I supposed to believe that? Look at me, living on the streets. If God loves me why doesn't he get me off the streets?"

Frank looked around the group waiting to see if anyone wanted to answer the question. When everyone remained silent, he turned toward Gus.

"Well, Gus, God's love doesn't really show up in fine clothes and comfortable lifestyles," he began. "But I can prove God loves you."

The man raised an eyebrow and grunted. "OK, prove it."

"Have you heard about Jesus?"

The man nodded.

"Jesus died for you, Gus, did you know that?" Frank asked.

"I've heard about that, but I guess it never really made much difference to me."

At that moment, Ruth began to speak. "If there hadn't been anyone else in the world, Jesus still would have died for you. He loves you that much," she said softly. "Of course it's up to you, whether you want to believe He's who He says He is. We all have the right to refuse His gift of eternal life."

Two of the other group members nodded in unison. "You know why He died, right?" one of them asked.

Gus shook his head. "Not really."

As the conversation progressed, Amber forgot the man's dirty condition and became deeply interested. Having been raised in a Christian home, she had never been around anyone who knew as little about God as this man apparently did. She took for granted that everyone had been exposed to the same type of upbringing she'd been given. She turned in her chair so she could get a better look at him.

"Jesus died to pay the price for our sins," Frank said simply. "Basically, because of Him you're a free man, Gus."

"A free man? I've always been free."

"Not really," Amber cut in, and the others looked at her in surprise. Then she turned toward Gus again. "When we're free in Christ, our circumstances don't really matter any more. All that matters is He is with us, He loves us, and He'll see us safely home in the end."

As Amber finished speaking, her words hit with a dramatic force. For weeks she had been complaining about the cramped quarters in the motor home and the other inconveniences of living on the road. Amidst her grumbling and complaining, she had forgotten the reason she had agreed to be part of the group. She hadn't chosen this lifestyle because of the comfortable surroundings or so that she could receive special treatment from others. Her purpose was only to tell people about Jesus. Now, this man sat beside her, hungry for the truth of a message she had understood since childhood. A wave of humility came over Amber, and she silently asked God's forgiveness for passing judgment on the man.

For the next thirty minutes the group shared with Gus stories from their lives, testimonies detailing how they knew for certain that God was near them. Finally, the man seemed to understand. He even wore a different look, as if there was hope in his life when only an hour earlier there had been none.

"Come with us," Frank said as the group prepared to leave. "We'll take you to the next town. There's a big church there and we'll set you up with someone who can help you."

Gus nodded absently, glancing at a clock on the wall. "Need to get to the bathroom first," he said, standing up and moving quickly toward the front entrance of the restaurant.

Frank and the others watched him go, and after less than a minute had passed, Frank stood up. "I'm going to make sure he's all right. He might need some help."

The others got up at the same time and agreed to meet Frank and Gus outside the restaurant entrance. After several minutes, Frank walked outside, wearing a baffled expression.

"I can't find him anywhere," he said. "He's not in the bathroom and I asked the cooks. He hasn't been back to the kitchen, either. He didn't walk out this way did he?"

The group members scanned the length of the street and shook their heads. "Haven't seen him," one member said.

Frank walked back into the restaurant and went up to the manager, whose desk was just inside the doorway.

"Have you seen a man with sort of old, ripped clothes and . . ."

"Oh, you mean the bum you brought in to eat with you?" the manager asked.

"Yes, did he walk out this way?"

"No. I've been here for the past half hour and he hasn't come this way."

Frank walked slowly outside, shaking his head. There were only three ways out of the restaurant—through the emergency fire door, which would have sounded a loud siren if it had been opened; through the kitchen loading door; and through the front entrance. No one had seen Gus near any of those exits.

"I can't understand it. It's like he just disappeared," Frank said, still scanning the restaurant hallway and looking out the front doorway up and down the sidewalk.

At that moment, Amber felt that she knew the truth. "You don't think, maybe . . ." she began and then grew silent. Her father had been a minister for years and believed in every truth the Bible taught. Because of that, there had been times when he talked about angels in his sermons.

"They're real," he had told his children one day. "Because God says they're real."

Frank looked at her a moment and then understood. "You mean, maybe he was an angel?"

Amber nodded.

Frank looked down the street again, searching for some sign of the man. "I guess we'll never know."

But suddenly Amber was convinced that God had sent the man to remind her of her purpose—not just her purpose while traveling with Departure, but her purpose in life. Today, whenever she sees someone less fortunate than she is, she remembers Gus and a Bible verse from Hebrews:

"Do not forget to entertain strangers, for by doing so some people have entertained angels without knowing it."

Badge-Bearing Angel

oshua Jones was trying desperately to stay awake. He had been the keynote speaker at a retreat in the mountains near Flagstaff, Arizona, and now, at 11:30 p.m., was driving the remote stretches of Interstate-17 back to Phoenix. It was very warm and his car's air conditioning had stopped working earlier in the week. The warm air and solitary highway were causing Joshua to nod off occasionally, and he was finding it nearly impossible to concentrate on his driving.

"Come on, Lord," he prayed aloud, his voice urgent. "Keep me awake. Just until the next rest stop."

Less than a minute later, Joshua saw flashing lights in his rearview mirror. There had been almost no traffic on the interstate for miles, and the area he was traveling was utterly remote. Joshua, who had been driving barefoot, struggled to put his shoes on as he pulled his car over, briefly wondering what a police officer was doing in this area. One thing was certain;

he was definitely wide awake now that an officer was pulling him over.

He stopped his car on the shoulder of the road, his shoes now on his feet, and watched in his mirror as the officer approached the car. He wore a standard highway patrol uniform but he was smiling. Joshua had only received two tickets in his life, none of them from smiling officers.

"Good evening, officer," Joshua said as the patrolman stopped beside his open window.

"Are you alright?" he asked, bending over a bit and looking at Joshua with searching eyes. Joshua noted his badge number: 37.

"Yes, fine."

The officer laughed. "At least you have your shoes on now."

Joshua looked puzzled. How had the officer known about his shoes? Before he could voice the question, the officer spoke again.

"You've been driving a long way and it's late. You almost fell asleep out there, didn't you?"

"Why, yes," Joshua stammered. "I was really struggling to stay awake. Maybe you can tell me where the nearest rest stop is."

"Better yet, I'll take you there," the officer said. "You spent the weekend helping everyone else, now it's your turn to get a little assistance. Follow me." The officer turned to leave.

"Wait!" Joshua cried. "Aren't you giving me a ticket or something?"

The officer looked at him evenly and shook his head. "No ticket. Just wanted to make sure you were all right. That's my job, you know."

Joshua nodded, distracted by the officer's strange comments. How had the patrolman known about the length of his trip or that he'd been helping people at the retreat? Joshua continued to consider the possibilities as he followed the officer back onto the highway and several miles south toward Phoenix. As he drove, he was pleased to realize he was no longer nodding off. The adrenaline burst, from being approached by an officer, had been enough to keep him awake for some time.

Finally the officer signaled that he was getting off at the next exit. As they approached the off-ramp, the officer exited first, taking a quick turn at the base of the hilly exit. As Joshua followed him, taking the same turn, he suddenly lost track of the motorcycle. He stopped his car and looked around. Directly ahead of him was a parking lot and a rest area complete with a gas station and all-night restaurant.

The setup was perfect. Joshua could stop for an hour or so, have some coffee and maybe a conversation with the officer, and be on his way without fear of falling asleep. He looked around, waiting for some sign of the patrolman. When he still couldn't see the officer, Joshua figured he was probably parking his motorcycle somewhere near the restaurant.

Joshua pulled into the parking lot, climbed out of his car and waited. After five minutes, he walked around the perimeter of the rest area, intent on finding the officer who had guided him to safety. Finally, he had searched every possible spot; the patrolman had vanished.

Years of work in Christian ministry, years of serving at his local church had not prepared him for the feeling that swept over him at that moment—suddenly he understood. There was only one way the officer could have known about Joshua's weekend and his bare feet.

The officer must have been an angel, sent by God to protect him from falling asleep. And Joshua was certain he would have nodded off within minutes if it hadn't been for the officer.

There was still one way to find out. Remembering clearly the officer's badge number, Joshua headed toward the all-night diner and walked up to a pay phone just outside the front door. He found the local highway patrol listed in the phone booth's Yellow Pages and dialed the number.

"I need to know the name of an officer," he told the receptionist. "He helped me out a little while ago and I want to thank him."

"Badge number?"

"Three, seven," Joshua said, remembering vividly each number as he had seen it on the officer's badge.

There was a pause. "Three, seven, is that all?"

"Yes."

"Are you sure?"

"Yes," Joshua said. "Positive."

"Well, you must be thinking of something else," she said strangely. "We don't have any officers with that badge number. Nothing even close. Our officers have numbers with three digits."

It was true, Joshua told himself as he hung up the telephone. From that moment on, Joshua believed that the officer had been an angel, sent to save him from certain death if he had fallen asleep while driving the interstate.

"Thank you, God," he said quietly, gazing toward the star-covered sky before climbing back into his car that night. "Thank you for protecting me."

Her Father's Face

oanie Everett had always been close to her father. When Joanie was a little girl growing up in Pennsylvania, Larry Everett would come home from work and spend hours playing with his little girl.

In the 1940s and 1950s, the two continued to be close as Joanie reached adolescence and then adulthood. They shared a love for athletics and the outdoors and often hiked around the lake near their home. Larry was his daughter's fiercest protector and the first one with a listening ear when she was at a crossroads in life. Their home was always a place of love and family fun.

Then, when Joanie was only twenty-five years old, her father became ill with cancer. He died a few months later. The loss of the man who had been such a central part of her life was overwhelming, and for months her mother worried about whether she would ever be the same again.

Since her father's death, Joanie had dropped out of college and did little more than clean the house and stay in the tiny bedroom she had grown up in. She also lost weight, and dark circles appeared under her once-bright blue eyes.

"Joanie, you need to get out of the house, meet people," Sarah Everett would tell her daughter. "Your father would never have wanted you wasting away like this in his absence."

Joanie knew her mother was right, but there was an emptiness inside her that she could neither escape nor explain. Months passed with little change in Joanie's depression. Then sometime near the anniversary of Larry's death, Joanie and two of her friends, Jill and Pamela, decided to hike along a lake that had been one of Larry Everett's favorite spots.

"I'm not sure we should be doing this," Joanie said as she and the others got out of the car and headed toward the lake. Parts of the hike would be hilly, and Joanie didn't feel she had the energy to scale the hills, not to mention the memories she would certainly encounter.

"Come on, Joanie. It's time," Jill said. She gently pulled Joanie's arm and led the slender, brown-haired young woman toward the trail.

Joanie nodded. "I know. Now or never." She took a deep breath and headed toward the lake, following her two friends.

For nearly thirty minutes, the threesome walked in silence, each lost in her own thoughts. Joanie forced herself to continue forward as the memories of her father bombarded her with an almost physical force. The three friends turned a corner to approach the steepest hill of the climb. The path followed the hill straight up and then leveled off along a fifty-yard plateau. At the top of the hill, a bench marked the spot where Joanie and her father had often sat and talked when they visited the lake.

Joanie swallowed hard and stared straight ahead. She would have to take the hill by storm, facing every memory along the way and refusing to give in to her overwhelming feelings of grief.

Then suddenly she saw someone on the hill high above her.

A tall man in a trenchcoat was standing on the plateau staring out at the lake. From her viewpoint, the man looked exactly like her dead father. Joanie gasped, but her friends did not seem to hear her, and the trio continued up the hill. As they did, Joanie kept her eyes on the man, and suddenly, she felt a burden being lifted from her shoulders. When they were just ten yards from the man, he turned toward Joanie and smiled the same warm and reassuring smile that had once belonged to Larry Everett alone.

Joanie's friends still seemed oblivious to the man and continued past him without stopping. When Joanie was only a few feet away from him, she paused and stared into his eyes. He winked once, smiled again, and then slowly turned back toward the lake.

At that instant, Joanie had no doubt that somehow this man was her father. There was no way anyone could look so much like him and be anyone else. She seemed to know, instinctively, that there was no need to question the man or engage in dialogue. A peaceful reassurance washed over her. She continued her hike, never even looking back at the man. Later, at the bottom of the hill, she asked her friends to stop a moment.

"Did you see him?" she asked. Immediately her friends noticed a different look in Joanie's eyes. Finally, after months of grieving, she seemed at peace with herself.

"Who?" Jill asked, with a blank look.

"Yeah, who?" Pamela said.

Joanie cocked her head curiously. "That man, up on the top of the hill." She turned and pointed toward the hill, but the man had vanished. "He was up there, near the bench."

Jill and Pamela assured Joanie that they hadn't seen anyone at the top of the hill. At that moment, Joanie felt another wave of peace and again somehow knew that it was not necessary to share the experience.

"Never mind," Joanie said quickly, resuming her walk. "Must have been my imagination."

Jill and Pamela shrugged; Joanie was thankful they dropped the subject. Whoever the man was, he had given her a glimpse of the father she so badly missed and the reassurance that she had desperately needed. She would keep the incident to herself for a while and savor it. And regardless of what anyone else would say to doubt it, from that point on Joanie was convinced that an angel bearing an uncanny resemblance to her father had been and would always be watching over her.

This notion was confirmed five years later when Joanie was working in Washington, D.C., near the Smithsonian Institute. She had gone into town for lunch and was returning along Tenth Street when she paused at the curb, waiting for the light to change.

Suddenly, she felt the firm grasp of a hand on her shoulder that pulled her back, away from the curb. The force from the hand was so strong, it nearly knocked her onto the ground. At the exact same instant, a city bus traveling along Tenth Street turned right at that intersection and jumped the curb directly where Joanie had been standing. If she had remained standing there, she'd have been killed.

She turned at once to thank the person who had rescued her, but there was no one within fifty feet of her. Again she felt an overwhelming sense of peace and reassurance.

Joanie is convinced that the person who saved her life was not of this world and that had she seen him, he would have borne a strong resemblance to her dead father.

Heavenly
Protection

ong before he and his wife, Jenny, traveled to New Hebrides Islands to spread God's word, the Reverend Stewart G. Michel felt drawn toward mission work. He had completed his education and training, and finally in 1973, he and Jenny had boarded a series of airplanes and moved to the islands.

"Are you afraid, Stewart?" Jenny had whispered as they arrived at the thatched-roof, single-room dwelling where they were to live and work as missionaries for the next year.

Stewart smiled calmly. Jenny was more concerned than he about the obstacles they would certainly face on the islands. Disease, deadly animals, and fierce natives all figured to play a factor in their lives for the next year. But Stewart was not worried, and he gently took Jenny's hand in his.

"Sweetheart, you know we'll be fine here," he said softly. "God will protect us."

Jenny nodded, looking anxiously at their surround-

ings. Everything seemed so foreign, so completely different than anything she'd seen before. There were no supermarkets, no paved roads,
nothing to offer the security she'd known all her life.

"You're worried, aren't you?" Stewart asked, squeezing her hand
and looking into her deep blue eyes.

Jenny laughed nervously. "Is it that obvious?"

"Yes," Stewart replied, with empathy. "Listen, I understand, really. But we have prayed for God's protection, Jenny. Do you believe
He hears us?"

Jenny nodded quickly. "Of course I believe."

"Well, then we have to trust. God brought us here for a reason,
and He's going to see us through."

They had shared the conversation a hundred times during their
preparation for this mission. But now, with their new home sitting just fifty feet away, there was something more real about the
reassurance Jenny felt. She smiled and climbed out of their beat-up
van, pulling Stewart along with her.

"OK, come on then," she had said, the hesitation gone from her
voice. "We have a mission to run!"

That had been six months earlier. They had learned to deal with
the disease, equipped as they were with various medicines and vaccines. And they had developed ways to stay clear from the wild
animals that lived in the brush near their home. Best of all, they
were finding ample opportunities to hold Bible studies throughout
the area and to teach the local tribes about their faith. But there
was one tribe—known for its fierce fighting techniques—which grew
more hostile toward them with each passing day. For weeks they
had threatened to attack the Michels and kill them because they had
interfered with ancient tribal traditions and taught their people a new
and strange way of thinking.

Finally, the hostile tribe made plans to carry out their threats.

Late in the evening of June 23, the Michels lay in their small bed and listened to the sound of war cries growing louder and louder.

"They're coming for us, Stewart," a terrified Jenny whispered in the dark of their bungalow.

Stewart nodded. "Keep praying, Jenny. Keep praying."

Jenny squeezed her eyes tight, trying to force the frightening sounds from her mind. But they grew still closer until their shrill screams and chanting surrounded the Michels's dwelling.

Stewart began to pray aloud.

"Heavenly Father," he began, "you have told us to ask for anything in your means. We come before you now and ask you to protect us as you have in the past. Please deliver us from the danger we are in."

For nearly an hour the sounds continued outside the bungalow. At the end of the hour, the Michels could see dancing lights surrounding their home.

"Fire," Stewart whispered, holding Jenny tightly. "Keep praying. I think they might try to burn us out."

Jenny gasped and buried her face in Stewart's shoulder.

Another fifteen minutes passed while the Michels continued to pray for protection. Then, suddenly, the screaming began to lessen and grow gradually more distant. "They're leaving!" Jenny said, and her muscles began to relax.

The couple lay listening in the darkness as the tribesman moved farther and farther away. Finally their menacing sounds disappeared altogether.

"Thank you, Father," Stewart said aloud, gazing toward the sky. "Thank you for protecting us. Thank you for delivering us."

Three months went by and the Michels had no explanation for why the tribesmen chose not to kill them that terrifying night. Then, in a strange turn of events, the chief of that tribe contacted the

Michels and began asking questions about their mission work and about Jesus Christ. Before the end of the year, the chief converted to Christianity. At that time Stewart Michel decided to ask the question that had burned in his mind for nearly a year.

"Why didn't you kill us that night?" he asked, staring gently into the chief's eyes.

The chief nodded. "We tried," he said. "But your guards wouldn't let us past."

Stewart's eyes narrowed in confusion. "What guards?"

The chief waved his arms dramatically. "Hundreds of guards, big men in shining clothes with swords drawn and torches," he said excitedly in broken English. But the missionary understood every word.

"Where did they come from?" he asked, baffled at the chief's story about what had taken place that awful night.

"Your guards," the chief repeated, as if the Michels should know where their protection came from. "Circled your hut, hundreds of them. Big men. Never seen anything like that before. We had no choice. We left."

Suddenly Michel thought he understood. Chills ran along his neck and down his arms. Hadn't they prayed for protection? Didn't God use angels as a way of taking care of his people? When Michel shared the story with Jenny, she agreed with him.

"God's protection came in the form of a hundred angels dressed like guards and stationed around our home," Jenny says when she talks of the event. "Who else could they have been but angels?"

Point
the Way

hen William Landemann set out for a hike around one of the frozen lakes near the University of Wisconsin at Madison, he knew nothing of the impending blizzard headed in his direction. At twenty-one years old, Landemann was an advanced hiker and backpacker with years of experience in the Great Lakes area hunting, fishing, and wandering the woods. He shared an off-campus apartment with two friends, and although he spent much of his time at school, he still preferred the solitude of the outdoors. It was only while outdoors, amidst undisturbed nature, that William felt truly connected with God.

Landemann had been raised a traditional Catholic but found the church to be too confining. He believed that God was bigger than weekly rituals and lists of rules, and when he was alone amidst nature he would spend hours praying and growing close to his Creator.

That cold February morning in 1975 was no different than many others like it. Landemann was in the habit of leaving the house without word to his roommates. He would spend most of the day alone in the wilderness that surrounded the edge of the university. He wore a down parka, boots, mittens, and a hat, planning his trip as he set out into the sub-zero morning. The lake was about a mile from the apartment. It was a beautiful lake, twenty-five miles in circumference, nine miles long, and about five miles wide. Landemann reached its frozen edge and decided to hike onto the lake. The water had been frozen for two months, and Landemann knew the ice would be quite thick. He guessed it would take about four hours to reach the middle of the lake and return back to shore.

When he had located a point quite a distance out which he deemed to be the lake's center, he began walking. As he trudged toward the middle of the lake, Landemann noticed people skiing, playing, and fishing through ice holes in the distance. He set his mind to prayerful thoughts and the effort needed to hike through the dense snow-covered ice pack. Landemann hadn't brought water that day, so about one hour into his walk he began to eat snow to quench his thirst.

Landemann was enjoying the hike immensely, taking in the beauty around him and feeling at peace with God and himself. As he reached the midway point and started to turn back toward shore, the sky began to cloud over. Landemann thought little of the cloud cover because it was so typical of the sky in Wisconsin during the winter. Many times the clouds would gather and then by morning disappear without any storm at all. Still, he picked up his pace, certain that if a storm was headed his way he would not want to be caught in it.

Minutes later, Landemann stopped for a moment and surveyed the encroaching weather formation. He was stunned by the change in the sky. Within minutes the clouds had grown dark and dangerously low, settling almost on top of the lake's frozen surface. Landemann could feel the temperature dropping, and as he picked up his pace, once again large snowflakes began filling the air. All at once, a fierce wind swept over the lake, swirling the snow flakes, and Landemann suddenly had trouble seeing the shore. Moving as quickly as he could against the wind, Landemann estimated a ninety-minute walk before reaching the shore. With the wind against him, the hike might take as much as two hours. He forced himself to move faster.

The wind continued to increase, and in only a few minutes, Landemann could barely see his hands in front of his face. The temperature had plummeted nearly thirty degrees because of the sudden storm. Landemann leaned heavily into the wind and continued to walk, losing track of time and pulling his arms close to his body in an effort to fight the effects of hypothermia. The blizzard grew even more fierce, and suddenly, Landemann stumbled onto the ice. When he opened his eyes, he realized he could see nothing but white. Even his hands had disappeared from sight. He fell in a heap, unable to move because of his sudden dizziness and inability to distinguish up from down. He was disoriented and could not move without falling. Then Landemann realized what had happened. He was snow blind.

In the years since he had first begun back-packing and exploring the forests near his home, Landemann had read about people who had been trapped in sudden blizzards and become snow blind. The condition was a deadly one, because once it happened, a person could become completely disoriented and freeze to death, sometimes only inches from safety.

Landemann pushed the thoughts from his mind and forced himself into a prone position on the ice.

"I've got to keep moving," he ordered himself aloud. "Keep moving!"

Reaching forward he dug his fingers into the snow and pulled his body forward. Now and then he would hear deep, powerful groans from beneath the lake's frozen surface.

"Help me!" he shouted, suddenly concerned that the ice would crack and he would drown in the freezing water. But his cries for help were swallowed up immediately by the force of the wind. At least he could move.

Time passed and Landemann was struck by another frightening thought. What if he had been crawling in circles, wasting valuable energy and getting no closer to the shore? He stopped and dropped his head onto the snow and ice, closing his eyes to shut out the horrifying blinding white that consumed him.

"Please, dear God, help me find my way!" he shouted. Tears filled his eyes and froze on his cheeks as he realized the gravity of his situation.

At that moment, Landemann heard the deep resonant sound of the foghorn which was located at the rescue station at the edge of the lake, just blocks from his house. For the first time in nearly thirty minutes Landemann had a reference point, a way to determine which way he was headed. Then he heard the sound of a voice speaking over the rescue station's private address system. "Be careful," the voice said clearly and loudly. "The breakwater is open and deep."

Landemann understood. He must have wandered close to the breakwater, where the ice was broken and the water, treacherously deep. He began slithering toward the voice. Again he heard a warning. "Be careful, stay to the right, climb the concrete wall when you reach it."

The voice pushed Landemann forward and filled him with hope. He knew if he could continue toward the voice and ultimately the rescue station, he would find safety. Soon he could hear the waves near the breakwater, and he obeyed the voice, staying to the right. Because he had used his hands to pull himself forward, he had lost nearly all feeling in them. But somehow, he reached the wall, still on his belly. He looked up, his body aching from exertion and the beginnings of hypothermia, and he saw the light from the rescue station ahead. He climbed over the retaining wall and felt his way through deep drifts of snow to the door of the rescue station.

A moment later the door opened, and he could feel himself being pulled inside by a large man. When Landemann had caught his breath and could open his eyes, the bearded man helped him into a chair and offered him a mug of hot coffee.

"Thank you," Landemann said, too stunned to say anything else, though his heart was full. Instead, Landemann stared at the man who had saved his life and was intrigued by his strangely peaceful nature.

The man moved to a table across the room and smiled at Landemann. "You were lost out there," he said softly, standing to refill Landemann's cup.

Landemann nodded. "Yes, I didn't know where I was. Couldn't see anything."

The man stared directly at Landemann. His eyes were crystal blue, a color Landemann had never seen before.

"Yes, I know. I knew you were lost so I sounded the foghorn. Then I sent out some advice about the breakwater, in case you had lost your bearings."

"Good timing," Landemann said, baffled at the way in which God had used this man to help him to safety.

As they spoke, Landemann realized that the weather had cleared up.

"Thank you again. I best be heading back," he told the man, who continued to sit at the table without any apparent task at hand. Suddenly Landemann was curious. "Why were you here, anyway?" he asked. Normally the lake's rescue station is closed down for winter.

"Doing research," the man said, smiling gently.

Landemann nodded, satisfied with the answer. He thanked the man again, the two said their goodbyes, and Landemann walked home. Not until he was safely inside his apartment did Landemann realize he had been gone for seven hours. He told his roommates about his experience.

"That's impossible," said Dana, one of Landemann's roommates. "The station closes down in the winter," she said absently. "Must have been some other building or something."

"No, it was the rescue station," Landemann said adamantly. "I know it's usually closed down by now, but this guy there really helped me. Said he was doing research or something."

His roommates looked at him doubtfully.

"The place has been closed down," Dana said once again. "I went by there the other day. Closed for winter."

"Listen, guys, I'm not losing my mind! I can still taste the coffee. Hey, he saved my life. He was there, and a good thing, too."

"I guess," Dana admitted. The roommates agreed that whoever the man had been, Landemann was certainly lucky he had been at the rescue station and seen him at just the right time.

After a long night's sleep, Landemann awoke the next morning determined to find the man and thank him again for saving his life. He dressed warmly and walked to the rescue building. As he approached, he suddenly grew confused. The station was locked tightly, its concrete-bunker design, lifeless and imposing. Puzzled, Landemann made his way to the front door, but found it nearly buried under a snow drift, which showed no signs of having been disturbed in weeks, if not months.

There had been no snow since the sudden storm the day before. The snow in front of the door should have been cleared away or, at least, there should have been obvious signs of tracks leading up and down the steps. Feeling more than a bit odd, Landemann dug through the drift to the door and found a sign which read: "Closed for winter (October 1975 to April 1976)."

But if the rescue station had been closed, locked with chains from the outside and partially buried under snow drifts, how had the man gotten inside? Furthermore, how had *he* gotten inside in the minutes after finding his way off the lake and out of the blizzard? Landemann stood motionless, going over the details of the day before in his mind. He knew this was the place he had come to. This was where the man had poured him hot coffee and helped him off the lake. The only foghorn in the area was located here at the rescue station.

Suddenly, Landemann knew there was one other way to check on the man's identity. He hurried home to call the county sheriff's department, which had jurisdiction over the building.

"No one has had access to the rescue station since it was closed down in the fall, Mr. Landemann," he was told. Landemann continued to search for information, dialing the local university to see if anyone had been given permission to do research at the building.

"No, the county doesn't allow any research at the rescue station during the off-season."

Landemann hung up the phone and fell to his knees, weak with the realization. Then he remembered his prayer and the way he had felt so close to God moments before the storm appeared.

"Could it have been?" he whispered to himself. "Is it possible?"

Although there would never be any way to prove what had happened that stormy afternoon, Landemann had made his mind up. From that point on, Landemann believed he had been helped by an angel who chose to save his life in what was a very special encounter.

Angel in a Yellow Snow-Removal Vehicle

n the winter of 1972, life was exactly what Dennis O'Neill wanted it to be. He had been preparing for the priesthood since graduating from high school, eleven years ago, and now he was just one year from his ordination. That winter, he was serving as a deacon for a parish in one of the northwest suburbs of Chicago, Illinois. His work kept him in constant contact with the parishioners, and he was developing a gift for helping people grow closer to God. He knew he had done the right thing by pursuing a life in the priesthood.

One evening, just before midnight, Dennis was driving southeast into Chicago during a blinding blizzard. As he reached the intersection of the Kennedy and Edens expressways—a crossing, where more than eight lanes of traffic come together—his car hit a patch of black ice and began to spin out of control.

Dennis bore down hard on the brakes but his car only spun faster, moving directly into heavy oncoming traffic. Although his car continued to spin violently,

Dennis managed to catch sight of a Volkswagon which was about to slam into his car. The other vehicle was so close, Dennis could clearly see its driver, even in the blowing snow. Dennis closed his eyes, bracing himself for what would certainly be a violent and painful impact.

"This is it!" he thought to himself.

But nothing happened. He opened his eyes slowly and found that his car had inexplicably stopped spinning. Directly in front of him was a large yellow snow-removal vehicle. The enormous truck-sized snow scraper had somehow protected Dennis from being hit by the Volkswagon or any other car. The driver, a middle-aged man with warm brown eyes and a baseball cap, motioned to Dennis that everything was all right and that he would shield Dennis's car until he was ready to resume driving.

Somehow, at the same time that he was stopped short and amidst utter confusion, Dennis experienced an unnatural silence. Even the traffic racing by on either side of him seemed to be making no noise. Dennis inched forward, turning his car in the right direction. Before driving away, he glanced in his rearview mirror and saw the driver of the snow-removal vehicle wave reassuringly. Dennis waved back and then drove away.

Moments later, his body began to shudder uncontrollably as he realized how close he had come to being involved in a severe car accident. The more he thought about the incident, the harder he began to shake, unable to understand what had happened. Where had the yellow vehicle come from? How had the cumbersome snowplow gotten between him and the oncoming cars? Why hadn't any of the cars crashed into him before the driver of the snowplow could position his vehicle safely in front of Dennis's?

Finally, as his body began to relax, Dennis realized there was only one answer. The hand of God had shielded him from certain death. With this realization, a feeling of peace washed over him.

Seven years passed and Dennis—by that time Father O'Neill—never forgot how God had helped him that cold winter night.

One day while serving as a priest at Saint Thomas the Apostle Church in Chicago, Father O'Neill asked a class of eighth-graders to share their personal experiences of how God had worked in their lives. As an example, he shared his story about the snow-removal vehicle.

"Ever since that winter of 1972, a snow-removal vehicle has been for me a symbol of God's love and protection," he told the wide-eyed group.

The next day, on an unusually warm and balmy May afternoon, Father O'Neill was driving a friend home from downtown Chicago when suddenly his right front tire experienced a blowout. Although it was the only blowout Father O'Neill had ever had, he knew how to change a tire; he carefully pulled his car off to the side of the road. As his car came to a stop, he glanced in the rearview mirror before opening the door.

There, pulling off the road behind him, was a large yellow snow-removal vehicle. Father O'Neill's eyes opened wide in surprise. He could not remember seeing any such vehicle on the expressway; there hadn't been an on-ramp for more than a mile. Father O'Neill remained in his car, watching the snow-removal vehicle and its driver, unable to imagine where either one had come from.

Slowly, the driver climbed out and walked up to Father O'Neill. He had warm, kind brown eyes and wore a baseball cap. He was smiling calmly. Before hearing him speak, Father O'Neill felt a silent reassurance coming from the man.

"Everything OK?" he asked.

"Yes, thanks," Father O'Neill said quickly. "Tire blew but I can change it."

"OK then, I'll be on my way," the man said, nodding his head and tipping the baseball cap. "I just wanted to make sure."

With that, the man turned around and climbed back into the snow-removal vehicle. As he drove away, he waved once more to the awe-struck priest.

To this day, Father O'Neill does not know exactly who the driver of the yellow snow-removal vehicle was or how such a large winter vehicle suddenly appeared on the Dan Ryan Expressway in late May. But he is as certain now as he was then that God is watching over him wherever he goes, using a number of means to assure his protection. Even, quite possibly, an angel at the wheel of a large, yellow snow-removal vehicle.

Christmas Angel of Hope

he story of hope was an integral part of Phyllis Scott's Christmas memories, and she would forever be touched when she shared it.

Back in 1911, when she was four and her brother, two, their parents, Jack and Martha, often struggled financially. Still, they shared an especially close bond and there was always enough food and love to go around.

That Christmas week was a troublesome one for the Scott family because Phyllis's little brother, Tommy, was sick; he had a high temperature and the doctors feared he might have polio. In those days, there were no vaccines for polio and many children died from that disease. Throughout the days and nights that preceded Christmas, Jack and Martha took turns kneeling by their sick little boy's bed and praying for his recovery.

In addition to the child's illness, there were other

troubles that Christmas. The mill where Jack worked had cut his hours in recent weeks, and they had been unable to afford Christmas presents for the children. Martha had been secretly knitting socks and scarves, but her dream of buying Phyllis and Tommy a toy each and some candy had been shattered. Now it was all they could do to purchase food and other necessities.

The Scotts spent Christmas Eve gathered in Tommy's bedroom praying and singing carols and sponging the boy's feverish body. After a long and restless night, the Scotts finally fell exhausted into their own beds.

Very early on Christmas morning, when Martha was up fixing breakfast and arranging the wrapped parcels of socks and scarves by the children's plates, she heard a loud knocking sound. Martha tilted her head curiously and wiped her hands on her apron as she moved toward the front door.

"Yes," she said as she opened it.

There, on the front porch, was a handsome, well-dressed man and a pretty little girl. A large white dog stood at the child's side.

"Merry Christmas, Mrs. Scott," the stranger said in a soft voice filled with kindness. "I've come to see how Tommy is doing?"

Martha stood staring at the man and child on her porch unable to comprehend how a stranger might know her name and the name of her child.

"Do I know you?"

The man ignored the question. "How is the child, Mrs. Scott?"

"Sir, who are you?" she asked. There was an unusual presence about the man and she was not afraid, but she wanted very much to know the identity of the stranger before her.

The man shook his head politely and smiled. "I came only to find out the condition of your son, ma'am," he said.

Still flustered, Martha ran her hand through her hair and took a deep breath and decided to answer the man. "Well, he's only a little boy, two years old," she began.

The man nodded kindly and the little girl beside him smiled. Martha continued.

"He's always been in good health until about a week ago when he caught this fever and—" she paused and her voice cracked. "Doctor says it might be polio."

"I know," the man said softly, reaching out toward Martha and squeezing her hand. "But he will recover shortly."

Tears began streaming down Martha's face, which she wiped away quickly. "Please, sir," she said, her face contorted in confusion. "Come in out of the cold and tell me who you are, how you know our names."

Again the man smiled and shook his head. "We must be going now," he said. "Close the door quickly so the cold doesn't get to the boy's room."

"But wait . . ."

The man waved once. Then he and the child and the big, white dog turned around and walked down the porch steps. Although he had cautioned her to close the door, Martha stood on the porch watching the trio to see where they were headed. Just as they reached the last step, Jack called out from the back room and Martha turned away. When she looked toward the porch again, the man, the little girl, and the dog had disappeared.

Martha ran quickly down the porch steps and scanned the street in both directions, but the sidewalks were empty. Dazed by what had happened, she walked slowly back into the house and shared the story with her husband.

"Who could he have possibly been?" she asked him.

"I don't know, Martha," Jack said. Then he smiled. "Maybe he was sent by God. A Christmas present to assure us that little Tommy is going to be all right."

The couple pondered this and before waking the children, they prayed again for their sick son.

"I'm going to check on Tommy," Martha said as she stood up from the table. "You get Phyllis and tell her to come downstairs for Christmas breakfast."

A few minutes later, when Jack was in Phyllis's room waking the girl and wishing her a Merry Christmas, he heard Martha.

"Jack, come quickly," she shouted.

Jack grabbed Phyllis's hand and the two ran down the hallway toward Tommy's room.

"What is it?" Jack was frightened; perhaps Tommy had grown worse or he might not have survived the night.

When they entered the little boy's room, Jack saw Martha sitting on the bed, her eyes glistening with unshed tears as Tommy sat grinning in her arms. She reached for her husband's hand.

"Jack, the fever's gone. He seems completely better," she whispered.

"Dear God," Jack whispered, and slowly, he knelt on the floor beside the child's bed. The Scott family held hands and thanked God for healing Tommy.

"And thank you, too, God, for the stranger this morning. Thank you for giving us hope."

They did not see or hear from the strange man again until three years later, in April 1914. This time he was alone, but when Martha answered the door, she knew instantly that this was the same man who had visited them that Christmas morning.

"You've come again!" Martha said, opening the door and waving an arm toward her living room. "Please come in. I want to know your name, who you are."

But just as before, the man smiled and shook his head. "I wanted to tell you I'm sorry about your husband losing his job. But he will be working again soon."

This time before Martha could say another word, the man smiled warmly, tipped his hat politely, and turned quickly to leave. Martha called after him and watched as he turned around the corner of the house and headed toward the thick woods in back of their home. Martha ran down the steps after him, but by the time she got to the back of the house, there was no one in sight and not a sound from anywhere. Again, the man had disappeared.

Shocked by his visitation, Martha returned to the house and convinced herself that she must have been imagining things. The man must have been a different person, and he must have had the wrong house. After all, Jack had not lost his job. She silently thanked God that her husband did, in fact, have a job, and tried to forget about the stranger at the door.

That night, Jack came home from work earlier than usual with his shoulders slumped in defeat. He pulled Martha slowly into a tight hug and then sat her down gently on their worn sofa.

"I have some bad news," he said, looking deeply into her eyes. "I was laid off today."

Martha felt her heart skip a beat at her husband's words. The stranger had been right after all. She sighed deeply and told Jack about the visit from the stranger earlier that day.

"He said you'd be back working again soon," she said as she finished the story. "Jack, who is he?"

Jack shook his head in awe. "Whoever he is, he seems to want to bring us hope. Remember that Christmas morning when we wondered if Tommy was going to make it? He already knew everything was going to be all right and wanted to give us the same peace of mind. Maybe it's true. Maybe we have nothing to worry about now, either."

Martha nodded. "Well, let's go eat dinner. At least for now we still have food on the table." She moved to take off her apron, then suddenly she gasped.

"Jack!" she screamed. "Look!"

In her hand, she held a twenty-dollar bill, which had been nestled in her apron pocket. "Twenty dollars, Jack! Where in the world did it come from?"

For a moment Jack and Martha were silent, and then, at the same time, both reached the same conclusion.

"The stranger?" Martha asked quietly. Jack nodded and took her hand.

"Maybe he was more than a stranger, Martha. Maybe he was our guardian angel. It's possible, isn't it?"

For days, the couple pondered the stranger and his message. Then, two weeks later, Jack's job was restored, and he was given a bonus check for returning to the position. After that, the Scotts were convinced that whoever the man was, he was neither human nor ordinary. He had known their names and their needs, and he had brought them hope in times of despair.

Each year until Martha died, her faith remained strong as she told the story of the stranger who came bearing hope. The Christmas angel, she liked to call him.

In many ways, the stranger is still spreading hope today, as the story, which now belongs to Phyllis, continues to be passed down among the children, grandchildren, and great grandchildren of Jack and Martha Scott.

Divine
Direction

r. Charles Madison had always wondered
what his life might have been like if he
had been a missionary. His parents had
known several missionaries, and as a boy,
Charles would listen to their stories, dreaming of someday traveling to far-off countries, where he could tell
people about the love of Jesus.

Instead, he worked his way through medical school
and became an emergency room doctor, working at a
hospital near his home, in Glendora. He never regretted
his decision to work in the medical field, viewing it as a
form of missionary work, in that he worked daily with
people and had been given numerous opportunities to
share his faith in the process. Regardless of his hectic
schedule, Dr. Madison always remained an active member of his local church, and by the early 1980s, he had
developed friendships with several missionaries.

When he was able to take some vacation time in
1981, Dr. Madison arranged a vacation to Bangalore, India, where he planned to visit his missionary

friends and experience their lifestyle.

"I'm just a little unsure about how to make the transfer when I stop in Bombay," Dr. Madison admitted to his friends in a final telephone call before making the trip. His air transportation took him through the Bombay Airport, where he would have to catch a connecting flight to Bangalore.

"Don't worry," his friends told him. "God will get you here."

When Dr. Madison boarded the plane in Los Angeles headed for Bombay, he recalled those words and wondered how the transfer would work out. He relaxed and didn't think about the situation again until the plane landed many hours later. He stood up and stretched, grabbed his carry-on bag, and made his way down a flight of stairs toward the main building.

Dr. Madison checked his watch as he entered the airport, which even at 4 a.m. was teeming with people. He had less than thirty minutes to catch his connecting flight to Bangalore. Walking to the first airline counter he could see, Dr. Madison smiled and began to speak.

"I'm looking for Flight 457, connecting from Bombay to Bangalore," he said slowly.

But the man shook his head quickly. "No," he fairly shouted. "No, no. No English!"

Dr. Madison understood by the man's gestures that he did not speak English. Glancing about the airport, Dr. Madison realized that although many people in Bombay speak fluent English, he could see no signs in English. He asked several more airline representatives, but after fifteen minutes, he still had no idea about which direction to go to catch his flight. He found his luggage but no one who could point him in the right direction.

Just when Dr. Madison began to wonder where he would go if he missed his plane, a man walked up to him dressed in standard American business clothing.

"Come this way," the man said in a voice that was authoritative but kind. The man turned his back on Dr. Madison and began walking.

"Hey, you don't know where I need to go," he yelled at the man, who was rapidly walking away. When the man did not respond, Dr. Madison shrugged and realized that he had no other options. He picked up his suitcase and followed the man. They walked the length of the airport, and the doctor followed the man outside where a bus was waiting at the curb.

"Get on here," the man said in the same commanding voice. When Dr. Madison climbed onto the bus, the man followed and took a seat opposite him.

"So, where are we going?" the doctor asked curiously.

"You need to catch a flight to Bangalore, correct?" the man asked in response.

Dr. Madison nodded, wondering how the man might have had that information.

"The domestic flights leave from the airport down the highway. The bus will take us there."

Dr. Madison nodded. "Where are you from?"

The man paused a moment. "I'm just home on break," he said.

Just then, the bus pulled up in front of the domestic airport.

"Hey, thanks a lot," Dr. Madison said appreciatively. "I would never have known about this place. No one around there spoke English."

"Yes," the man answered, glancing out the window. "I know. You'll be fine now."

Dr. Madison walked toward the door of the bus and stepped out, reaching up into the bus's luggage rack located on the outside of the bus next to the passenger door. He waited a moment for the man to follow him, but when no one came out Dr. Madison, stepped back inside the bus.

The man was gone.

Dr. Madison moved backward and stood beside the bus completely stunned. The man definitely had not left the bus; Dr. Madison had been standing beside the exit and would have seen him. But where had he gone? And how had he known exactly where he needed to go to catch his flight? Another thing bothered Dr. Madison. If he was an American, how could he be home on break in India? The doctor stepped inside the bus once more and looked carefully around, making certain the man was not still inside. Finally he shook his head, picked up his suitcase and caught his connecting flight to Bangalore.

Once he had arrived and was seated around the kitchen table with his missionary friends, he shared his story.

"Maybe he was an angel, Charles," one of his friends said, his voice serious.

Dr. Madison was quiet for a moment. "I never thought about it. But I guess it's possible."

"Of course it's possible. God works in strange ways sometimes."

After that, Dr. Madison put the incident behind him. He was never sure whether the man had actually been an angel, but at the same time he had no other explanation for his assistance and then disappearance. In the years that followed, Dr. Madison's practice grew busy as did his personal life. He got married and was very satisfied with the direction his life was taking. He did not think about the incident in Bombay until about four years later when he decided to visit the same missionary friends, who by then were in Kenya.

This time his travels took him through the Pakistan airport. He got off the plane and was instantly in the familiar situation of look-ing for an English-speaking person to guide him toward the right terminal. None of the signs were in English, and Charles suddenly remembered his experience in Bombay as if it were only a day or so ago. He set his suitcase down and looked around, desperately searching for someone to give him directions.

Suddenly, a man dressed in traditional Indian garb approached him.

"You need to go this way," the man said, speaking in perfect English. He pointed toward a nearby terminal where travelers were lining up and about to board an airplane. Dr. Madison picked up his luggage and turned to thank the man. As in Bombay, the man was suddenly gone. Dr. Madison stood stuck in place, chills running down his spine. The man could not have gotten away so quickly.

Later that evening, when the doctor arrived in Kenya, he wasted no time in sharing the event with his friends, this time suggesting to them that the man had indeed been an angel.

"Remember the man who helped me in Bombay?" Dr. Madison asked.

"Sure, he steered you in the right direction and then disappeared, right?"

Dr. Madison nodded. "Well, you were right about him, because it happened again."

"You mean about him being an angel?"

"I have no doubt. God is really something, isn't he? Helping me out like that when I felt completely lost."

"Nothing new about that, my friend," one of the missionaries said, a smile covering his face. "If only we will listen, God will always points us in the right direction."

Dr. Madison was silent a moment, thinking of how he had felt guided into a medical career and of the other events in his life. He had grown up believing God was always watching over him. But now he had a different, more real understanding of that truth. "You know," he said, his eyes warm with the knowledge of God's very real presence. "I think you're right."

Miracle in the Mundane

hat warm June in 1993 had been hectic, and it seemed that Caryn Lessur had been late for nearly every appointment she'd made that week. Her husband, Donny, a high school teacher, was in his last week of instruction at the private school where he taught in West Hills. It was 2:10 in the afternoon and Caryn knew she had to pick her husband up at school by 2:30.

"I only need a few things," she told herself aloud as she pulled into the parking lot of the grocery store, across the street from the school. Gently lifting her four-month-old son and grabbing her wallet, she dashed into the store. Once inside, however, she found several additional items the family needed and quickly filled a cart with groceries.

With the baby's carrier in one cart, she needed two carts to get all the bags out to the car. A market clerk offered to push one of them.

With only two minutes before she was to meet Donny, she hurried to open the car's trunk, directing the clerk to place the bags inside.

"Thanks for the help," Caryn said, smiling as she took her tiny son from the other cart and strapped him in his seat inside the car. As she was doing so, the clerk took both carts and began pushing them back toward the store.

"I'll take care of the carts," she yelled toward Caryn, who was still getting her son situated. "Have a good day."

"Thanks," Caryn said, and then slipped into the front seat. At that moment she realized that she had left her wallet on the top seat of one of the shopping carts. She turned around and saw that the clerk had gone inside. There was no telling where the cart was.

Glancing at her watch, Caryn took her son out of the car once again and ran back into the store toward the clerk.

"My wallet, did you see it?" she asked, out of breath and nervous.

A blank look fell upon the clerk's face. "Wallet?"

Caryn nodded frantically. "It was on the top seat of the cart. Where'd you take them?"

The clerk pointed outside. "Out there with the others."

"OK. Thanks."

Caryn rushed outside, still holding her baby, and looked at the long row of carts. She quickly guessed that there might be as many as a hundred carts lined up in front of the store. Still, the cart would have to be near the front or back of the line because only a few minutes had passed. She raced toward the front of the line of carts and began looking inside each one. The wallet was not to be found.

Frustrated and aware that she was already ten minutes late for Donny, Caryn went back inside the store and asked about the wallet at the store's lost-and-found section.

"Nothing's been turned in, ma'am," the girl said. "Can I get your name and number? We'll call you if we find anything."

Caryn nodded quickly and jotted down the information. Then she began racing through the store asking each shopper if they had taken a cart from outside and if they had found a wallet in it. But each time she asked the question she met with the same blank expression. No one had seen her wallet.

Finally, Caryn and her son returned to their car. As she drove across the street toward the school, Caryn made a mental checklist of everything the wallet contained: her driver's license, credit cards, her children's medical cards, numerous receipts, her automatic banking card, personal mementoes, and a book of checks. But most important of all, it contained a special picture of her and Donny taken when they were dating. Caryn began to pray.

"Lord, if there's any way, please let someone kind find my wallet so I can get it back," she prayed. "And help me to slow down."

Twenty minutes late, Caryn pulled up in front of the school and explained the entire story to her husband. The couple had been faithful Christians for six years and Caryn wasn't surprised by her husband's words.

"I'll pray about it, too, honey," he said. "Everything will work out just fine."

"How can it?" Caryn cried. "That wallet is old, and my favorite picture of us is inside. It means so much to me, and I know I'll never see it again."

"Come on, honey. Have faith!"

Over the years, whenever Donny had reason to use those words, Caryn had been amazed at the ways God had worked out their problems. He had always provided for them, but still, at times like this, she would sometimes doubt that God could truly help.

"I feel funny asking God to help me find my wallet," Caryn admitted. "These things happen. And anyway, it was my mistake. Maybe He's trying to teach me a lesson. Telling me to slow down."

Donny shrugged and pulled her close. "Could be," he said. "Either way, things will work out. Stop worrying."

That night Caryn made several telephone calls to cancel her credit cards. But she knew there was a greater danger someone would use the driver's license and checkbook. The phone call to the bank would have to wait until business hours the next day. And she was miserable over her lost photo.

Early in the morning, Caryn called the market and asked if anyone had turned in a wallet. They hadn't, so next, she called the bank and was told to come in as soon as she could. The checking account would have to be closed and a new one opened.

"You'll have to fill out several forms, then we'll close your old account. We'll make a note that the wallet was stolen, in case there are any checks written by someone other than you or your husband. Then you can open a new account and transfer the old balance," a bank teller explained over the telephone.

Caryn called Maria, a church friend who sometimes babysat for her children, and asked her to come over to babysit for an hour. When she arrived, Caryn picked up her keys and headed for the door. "Pray for me, Maria. I'm still hoping that somehow the wallet will turn up."

Caryn drove to the bank's branch where she had originally opened the bank account, even though that location was farther away than others. She sat with a bank officer for twenty minutes filling out forms. Then she was directed to wait in line for the next available teller, who would arrange a cash advance until her money could be transferred from the old account to the new.

Caryn thanked the woman and moved into line. When it was her turn, she walked up to the next available teller. As she began to explain the situation, the woman held up an object and Caryn gasped.

It was her wallet.

"How did you get it?" Caryn asked, confused and elated at the same time.

"Happened a few minutes ago," she explained. "Two young men walked in, came up to my window, and handed me the wallet. I asked them their names, but they didn't want to give them to me."

Caryn's mind raced in search of an explanation. The bank had not been busy that morning, and she had watched the customers come and go. She hadn't seen any young men in the building. Also, she had lost the wallet at a market at least seven miles away, completely across town.

Caryn took the wallet and examined it carefully. Everything was intact; not even a single credit card or receipt was missing. And the treasured photo was just where she kept it tucked, Donny's face smiling at her as they watched the sunset over Lake Tahoe that summer so many years earlier.

As she drove home, Caryn thought about Donny's faith and the way he and she had prayed about the situation. Then she thought about what had happened. The wallet had been taken by someone almost immediately after she'd lost sight of it. Caryn had spoken with every shopper at the market and looked through every cart, and since no one ever turned the wallet in at the store's lost-and-found area, the person who originally took the wallet was obviously dishonest. How, then, Caryn wondered, did the wallet wind up in the hands of the two men who returned it to the bank? And how had they known which branch to take it to? Furthermore, how was it that at the exact time Caryn was in the bank, the men had returned the wallet and handed it to the specific teller who would later wait on her?

Later when she shared the story with Donny, his eyes lit up in a knowing way. "Prayer, sweetheart."

"What about those guys?" she asked, puzzled but convinced, just as her husband was, that finding the wallet was an answer to prayer. "I know no one walked in with my wallet while I was there."

"Remember what the Bible says about angels?" Donny asked, raising one eye.

Caryn paused a moment, allowing his words to sink in. "Is it possible?" she asked, her voice filled with awe.

"What do you think?"

Neither Caryn nor Donny would ever know for sure how Caryn's wallet was returned in such an unlikely set of circumstances. And they would never know the identity of the two men who performed perhaps an angelic service amid the mundane routine of everyday life.

Unseen
Angels

he following story was told at Lake
Avenue Congregational Church in Pasadena, California, in conversation during a
Sunday school class. As with several other
tales told here, the names and certain details have
been changed to protect the identity of the people
involved. But there is something different about this
story. Whereas other angel encounters in this collection
involve interaction with people who quite possibly were
angels, this story does not. Still, it is my opinion that an
angel encounter of some kind took place, and I wanted
to share it with you.

Christine Hallberg had finished shopping and was
discouraged to see what time it was. The southern
California mall had announced its closing message and
now it was after nine o'clock. Christmas was still less
than a month away, and Christine had hoped to get a
great deal of shopping done before the rush began in
earnest.

She gathered her bags in her arms and dug through

her purse for her car keys. She knew she needed to hurry. Her husband, Mike, was home with the boys and would have been expecting her by now. Walking outside the mall into the dark, cold parking lot, Christine continued to fumble through the belongings on the bottom of her purse in search of her car keys.

Lost in her search, she did not notice the movement of at least one person very near her car.

Finally her fingers wrapped around her keys and she looked up for her car; the parking lot was nearly empty. She realized in dismay how far away she had parked. Glancing around nervously, she picked up her pace. Ten years ago she might not have worried about her safety in such a situation. But now, in 1991, crime had increased in all parts of Pasadena and the surrounding areas. Christine knew she was in a vulnerable position as she made her way to her Buick, opened the door, and climbed inside.

Suddenly, a masked man appeared less than ten feet from her window. His eyes were wild and he was walking toward her, pointing a gun at her, and motioning for her to open the door.

Resisting the urge to panic, Christine ignored the man, locked her door, and tried to start her car. Nothing happened. The man was nearly at her door; she tried again, but the engine seemed to be completely dead.

"Please, God!" she whispered, just as the man began banging the handle of the gun on her window.

Closing her eyes, Christine tried once more to start the car, and finally, the engine turned over. In an instant, Christine slammed the car into gear and sped off, leaving the man in the shadows.

Christine cried the entire way home, stunned by what could have happened and baffled by her car's refusal to start the first time. The car had just been thoroughly inspected and had passed with flying colors.

She turned her thoughts toward God and thanked Him profusely for helping her out of what so easily might have been a life-threatening situation. She shuddered as she imagined what the man might have done if she had been stuck there just a few moments longer. Especially with the parking lot dark and most of the Christmas shoppers already gone.

She pulled into the driveway of their hillside home minutes later and, still feeling weak from the ordeal, made her way inside. There she tearfully shared the incident with her husband.

"You're safe now," Mike told her, taking her into his arms. After Christine had told him the specific details of the incident and what the man had looked like, Mike called the police. Once that was done, he turned to his wife.

"Let's go outside and look at the car," he said. "I can't understand why it would have done that. The mechanic just checked it out a few weeks ago, right?"

"Right," Christine said, nodding.

"I don't get it," Mike said, grabbing a flashlight and leading Christine outside toward the car. She watched as he opened the hood. Suddenly he stood back, allowing the flashlight to drop slowly by his side. He looked stunned, and Christine looked instantly concerned.

"What's wrong?" she asked.

"It's impossible," he muttered.

"What?" Christine moved closer, looking into the car's engine.

"There," Mike said, pointing the flashlight once more at the engine. "The battery is gone."

"What," Christine was confused. "How could it be? I just got home."

Mike turned slowly toward his wife. "Don't you see? Someone set you up. While you were shopping, someone took your battery and then waited for you. They knew you wouldn't be able to start your car and . . ." Mike stopped mid-sentence imagining what the masked man had intended for his young, beautiful wife.

"It's impossible," he said again.

"I don't understand," Christine said. She was more confused than ever, and terrified at Mike's discovery. She had been set up and somehow escaped being attacked. "If the battery is gone, how did the car start, Mike?"

"That's what I mean. There isn't any way to start an engine like this without a battery."

Chills made their way down Christine's spine and she reached for her husband's hand. "What are you saying?" she asked softly.

"I don't know. I can't explain it. Somehow you made it home without a battery. It's impossible."

Suddenly Christine felt a peace wash over her. "Mike, could it be God was watching out for me?"

Mike's eyes widened and a knowing look came over his face. Slowly, deliberately, he stared up at the star-covered sky. Christine followed his example, and for several minutes the couple gazed into the night. Finally, Mike broke the silence.

"God, we may never understand what happened tonight," he whispered. "But we are eternally grateful. Thank you."

Glimpse of a Guardian Angel

ll of the children in the Roman family walked a straight and narrow path. Their parents, Candelario and Leonor, were born in Puerto Rico in the early part of the century. They had always taught their children to have self-respect, a kindness toward others, and a devotion to God. The Roman children grew up in the late 1950s and 1960s, in the borough of Manhattan in New York City on the Upper West Side, an area that at that time was often dangerous.

For that reason, the children had strict orders to come home immediately after school. One of the few places the children were allowed to play and participate in after-school activities was the Holy Name of Jesus Catholic Church on Ninety-sixth Street and Amsterdam Avenue. As a result, each of the eight Roman children grew up with a strong faith and a sense of morality that has lasted to this day.

Of all the Roman children, Linda, the youngest of the five girls, was perhaps the most devout. From a young age, she had a sense of responsibility and a desire to care for those who could not care for themselves. She was by her mother's standards the classic "good girl," and she grew up living what her family considered to be a charmed life. But there was something else that set Linda apart from her siblings. They believe Linda had a childhood guardian angel who made at least two appearances to her family members.

The first incident happened in 1966, when Linda was five years old. At that time, she slept in the same bedroom as two of her sisters, Carmen and Cookie, ages ten and twelve. The older girls did not mind sharing their space with Linda, because they felt it was their job to watch over her.

One night, long after the lights had been turned out and Linda had fallen asleep, Carmen and Cookie were still whispering to each other when they thought they heard something. Looking up, they glanced at Linda and there, lying in her bed beside her, was a little girl of about the same age. For nearly a minute, the girls stared at the stranger in Linda's bed, exchanging looks of surprise, unsure what to do next.

Suddenly, the older girls slipped back under the covers, afraid that perhaps they were seeing a ghost or that if they turned away the strange little girl might become a monster. Eventually, Linda's frightened older sisters fell asleep, snuggled together under their bed covers. In the morning the little girl was gone and Carmen and Cookie were baffled.

"Mommy," Carmen approached their mother before breakfast that morning. "Linda had a little girl sleeping with her last night and today she's gone."

The children's mother paused for a moment, wiped her hands on her apron, and looked thoughtfully at her daughter. "What do you mean, honey?"

"Last night me and Cookie were awake and we looked over at Linda's bed. There was a little girl sleeping right beside her. This morning she's gone. Who was she?"

Her mother paused again and tilted her head. Then she smiled. "I guess it was her guardian angel," she said.

Linda woke up shortly after and joined her family in the kitchen. Although only five years old, Linda knew instantly that her family was talking about her. When she asked her mother what her sisters were discussing, Leonor took the girl aside quietly.

"It's nothing to be scared about, honey," her mother said gently. "The girls saw an angel near your bed last night."

Linda thought about her mother's words for a moment and then nodded in understanding. "A good angel, Mommy?" she asked.

"Of course," her mother answered.

Although neither she nor anyone else in the Roman family knew why Linda might have needed a guardian angel, with the constant dangers of the inner city the angel's presence was more comforting than curious. After that neither Linda nor her mother gave much thought to the incident. For Leonor, it was almost as if, in her deep faith, she was not terribly surprised that an angel might be watching over her children. Carmen and Cookie, however, talked about Linda's angel often, telling the story to their brothers and sisters on a regular basis and checking in on her at night in hopes that they would see the angel once more.

But years passed before the mysterious little girl was seen again. This time, Linda was a junior at a private girls' high school near their New York City apartment. By then, Linda had grown up quite close to her youngest brother, Joey. Each day at 3:30 p.m. Joey would wait anxiously in anticipation of his sister's return from school. Then the two would play together, listening to the radio and sharing secrets for hours. One afternoon Linda's mother looked through the peephole of their apartment door and saw that Linda had just gotten off the elevator and was heading toward the door with a friend in tow.

"Joey, Linda's coming. She's got a friend with her," she yelled toward the back of the apartment, where Joey had been in his room playing.

The twelve-year-old boy came running at full speed toward the front door. He grabbed the nearest chair and stood up, looking through the peephole just as his mother had done minutes earlier.

Walking with Linda was a young girl who appeared to be sixteen or seventeen, the same age as Linda. She was dressed in the same school uniform and she seemed extraordinarily happy. Joey had never seen the girl before, and something about her brilliant blond hair caused him to stare. Then, as if she could sense his eyes on her, the girl darted playfully behind Linda, peeking her head out every few steps.

Joey climbed down from the chair, unlocked the apartment door, and waited as Linda opened it. Joey strained to look behind his sister but the blond girl had disappeared. Linda was all by herself.

"Hey, where's your friend?" Joey asked, suddenly confused as he stepped out into the hallway and peered up and down its length.

Linda looked strangely at her younger brother. "What friend?"

"You know, the girl who was with you. Where did she go? Come on, Linda!"

Linda shrugged, walking past Joey and putting her books down on the kitchen table. "I walked home by myself."

Joey caught up to his sister, took hold of her arm and turned her to face him. "This isn't funny, Linda. She was walking right beside you. Then she moved behind you, kind of like she was playing around or something. She had long blond hair and she had the same uniform as you. Where is she?"

At that moment Leonor walked into the room. "Where's your girlfriend, Linda?" she asked simply.

Linda wrinkled her face in confusion. "What girlfriend? I came home by myself."

"But I saw her . . ." Leonor's voice trailed off and she appeared to be deep in thought. There was silence for a moment. "There wasn't anyone with you?"

"No one, Mom."

The confusion in her face disappeared instantly. "Your guardian angel," she said plainly, having reached what was for her an obvious conclusion. She smiled at Linda and turned back toward the kitchen, where she had been preparing dinner.

Like the first time, when Carmen and Cookie had seen the strange little girl sleeping alongside their sister, Leonor never mentioned the incident again. Even Linda rarely talked about the times her family had seen the mysterious girl by her side. Now, at age thirty-seven, Linda still has never seen the girl she believes to be her guardian angel.

"But I have always had a special feeling of protection," says Linda, now happily married and with two beautiful children. "As if I knew for sure that God was looking out for me."

As for Joey, at thirty-two he remains baffled by the experience that afternoon, an event that has strengthened his faith and given him direction in life.

"I know I saw someone with Linda that day," he says. "Can she have been anyone but a guardian angel?"

A Message of Hope

he market colors began changing while Jim Marlin was shopping for groceries. He had promised his family that he was finished with drugs. But in the San Fernando Valley of Southern California, where he lived, drugs were so easily accessible that he had once again been unable to resist. He had taken a mixture of illegal drugs hours earlier, and now, suddenly, the walls of the market seemed to be melting, their colors running into each other.

Jim looked around desperately, trying to steady himself, and aware that sweat had begun pouring from his forehead, dripping down his face, neck, and arms.

"Not now," he whispered out loud. "Please not now."

He turned toward the produce section, but the fruit and vegetables had turned into large bloblike substances and worse, they were coming toward him.

"Help!" he screamed and began running full speed through the store, up one aisle and down the next.

Finally, alerted by concerned customers, the store manager and one of the customers, a strong, well-built man in his late twenties caught Jim and forced him to the ground.

"Hold his feet," the customer said calmly, directing the store manager toward Jim's legs. "I've got his arms."

In the middle of a terrible drug-induced hallucination, Jim writhed violently on the floor trying to free himself from the grasp of the men who held him down. The hallucination was getting worse.

Every time Jim opened his eyes, he saw horrible, dark demons coming toward him. They had fierce expressions and fangs that dripped blood. There were small, evil demons floating near his face and laughing at him, and there were huge, monstrous demons circling him. Worse than the way they looked, the demons seemed to be emanating a sense of utter evil, a death and destruction that Jim was powerless to escape.

"Help me, someone help me," he shouted. "They're trying to kill me."

The customer, who had been holding Jim's arms, leaned in closer to him.

"You're going to be OK," he said in a voice that was soothing and clear. Despite Jim's severe hallucinations, he could hear the man and he began nodding.

"Help me!" he shouted again.

"Open your eyes, Jim," the customer said calmly in a voice only Jim could hear. He appeared to be unaware of the gathering of people that had encircled them. "Come on, Jim, you can trust me."

Jim opened his eyes slowly, then as the picture became clearer, his eyes grew wide in astonishment. The demons were still there, but they were retreating. And in the center of the picture was what appeared to be the face of Jesus Christ. Awestruck, Jim stopped twisting and struggling and suddenly grew calm.

As he stared, the image in the center of the picture began to speak. "Do you want to be free from the demons, Jim?" the voice of the Christlike image asked. "You need to decide."

Suddenly, Jim began to cry, and the crowd, which had grown even larger, watched as the young man continued to lean over him, talking in a voice none of them could hear.

"Yes," Jim cried softly. "Help me get rid of the demons. Please, help me!"

The man in the picture smiled gently. "No more drugs, Jim. With them come the demons. It is your choice."

"No, I can't do it by myself," Jim screamed, and the people surrounding him and the customer who spoke to him began to fidget restlessly. There was something unreal about the conversation these two seemed to be having. Even though they still could not hear the quiet words of the man.

Jim had closed his eyes again and once more started to struggle out of the stranger's grasp. But the man seemed to possess an inhuman strength and Jim's efforts were futile.

"Look at me, Jim," the gentle voice said again. "Trust me."

Slowly, Jim opened his eyes again. This time the demons were gone completely. Only the image of a very pure and radiant Christ filled the center of his vision.

"Help me," he whispered weakly. "Please."

"Jim, you won't have to do this by yourself. If you want to be rid of the demons, turn to me. I will always be right here to help you. Just call me and I will be with you."

"Lord?" Jim whispered the word, not sure if he was still hallucinating, but savoring the peace he felt all the same.

Slowly the image began to fade. But before it disappeared altogether, he heard the voice once more. "Yes, Jim. It is I. I will be here for you."

Suddenly Jim felt extremely tired. He closed his eyes and his body went limp. The customer who had been talking quietly to Jim and holding down his arms stood up.

"I think you can handle it from here," he said softly. "The worst of it is over."

"Thanks," the manager said, moving quickly toward Jim's arms and pinning the sleeping man down in case he awoke again. When the manager looked around to ask the customer what he had done to calm the man, the customer had vanished. At that moment, paramedics arrived and the manager stepped back so they could begin working. The police had also arrived, and the commotion was growing by the moment.

"Excuse me," a woman said as she made her way to Jim. "I'm his wife. Please let me see him."

Jim's wife, Jennika, a pretty, dark-haired woman with tears in her eyes, moved next to Jim and watched as paramedics took his vital signs.

"Seems to be OK, now," one of them said. "Drug hallucination?" he asked, staring at the store manager.

"Yes, definitely. Never seen anything like it."

Jennika closed her eyes and began crying again. Jim had promised her his days of doing drugs were behind him. He had been in and out of a rehabilitation center twice in the past two years, and she was beginning to wonder if he would ever quit. The paramedics had backed away from Jim, having determined that he needed no immediate medical attention. As they moved away, Jennika moved in close to Jim's head.

"Jim, sweetheart, wake up," she whispered. "Come on, get up, honey."

Immediately Jim opened his eyes. "Where is he?" he asked.

Jennika was confused. "Who?"

Jim sat straight up and looked around until he saw the manager. "Where did he go, that man who was holding me down?"

The manager glanced at the crowd, which had dwindled to just a few people. "I guess he's gone."

Slowly, Jim rose to his feet. At that instant, a policeman moved in and placed handcuffs on Jim's wrists as he read him his rights. Because his hallucination had happened in a public place, the police were arresting him for making a public disturbance. In addition, they were concerned for his safety and the safety of those customers around him.

Before the police led him away, Jim turned again to the manager. "Please," he said, suddenly much calmer than he had been moments earlier during the hallucination. "Tell me what that man looked like."

The manager squirmed uncomfortably at the strange request. "He was, well," the manager began, trying to remember. "He had short blond hair, muscular build and, let's see, well, a real clean-shaven face. That's all I can remember."

Jim shook his head. "No, I mean the other man. The one who leaned over me and talked to me."

"Yes, that's who I'm telling you about."

"No, the man who helped me. He had dark hair, a beard, brown eyes. Where is he?"

The manager did not know what to make of Jim's statement. He had no experience with hallucinogenic drugs and no way of knowing what Jim had seen during the violent episode.

"All I can tell you is that the man who helped you was a blond guy," the manager said.

Jennika had been listening to the exchange between her husband and the store manager and was very curious about what Jim had seen and heard during his hallucination.

"Are you alright, Jim?" she asked.

Jim looked from the manager to his wife in frustration. "No one knows where he went?" he asked.

"No. He left right after you calmed down," the manager said. "Look, let's get this thing cleaned up. I've got a store to run here."

The policeman nodded and led Jim outside to the waiting police car.

"Something happened in there," he said, looking into his wife's eyes as he was ushered into the car. "My life will never be the same again, Jennika."

He saw the frightened look on her face, unsure of what to make of his statement.

"Don't worry, love," he said, smiling through tears. "I'll tell you everything later."

Jim was booked and released from the police station after promising to appear in court to deal with his public disturbance charge. Jennika picked him up at the station later that afternoon. Normally after he'd gotten into trouble because of his drug use, Jim was angry and defiant. But as Jennika watched him approach their car and climb inside, she saw that he was strangely upbeat.

"Are you going to tell me what happened back at the grocery store?" she asked, making no move to start the car and giving Jim her full attention.

"Yes," he said, staring out the window at the blue sky above. He turned toward Jennika. "Jen, do you believe God might be trying to tell me something?" he asked.

Jennika sighed. She was dying to know what had happened in the market and Jim seemed bent on delaying the discussion.

"Of course," she answered patiently. Jennika was a prayerful Christian who asked God daily to help Jim stop doing drugs. Lately she had prayed that he would use whatever means necessary to reach

Jim and help him to give his life over to God.

"Now please tell me what happened at the market," she begged.

"I'm not sure you're going to believe me, but I'll tell you. I did some drugs earlier and then I went shopping. Just had the munchies I guess," he began. "Then I began to hallucinate, everything was turning different colors and it seemed like the vegetables were coming to life." Jim glanced at his wife and was relieved to see that she wasn't laughing. She had never found any humor in his hallucinations, only disgust and sadness that they had been brought on by his drug use.

"Well, I began sweating and then I think I started running through the store screaming for help," he said. Jennika's eyes narrowed in pain, sorry she hadn't been near her husband to help him. "Well, I began to see black beings in the air and I closed my eyes. I think I just stood there screaming for help. When I opened my eyes, there were demons; that's the only way I can describe them. They were all around me—black beings with fangs and claws and blood dripping from their mouths. Oh, Jennika, it was so horrible."

Jim hung his head for a moment, reliving the nightmare of the hallucination. Jennika reached over and took his hand.

"Honey, tell me what happened next."

Jim nodded. "Well, I felt someone grab me and then someone was holding my feet and someone else was holding my arms. I had my eyes closed and I was still screaming. Then, all of a sudden I can hear this calm, gentle voice telling me to open my eyes and to trust him. Now, here's where it gets really weird. I opened my eyes slowly and the demons were leaving, they were moving away as fast as they could. And in the center of the picture was a man who looked exactly like the pictures of Christ I've seen. He was holding my arms gently and speaking softly so that only I could hear him."

"Did he say anything?" Jennika asked, mesmerized by the story Jim was telling.

"Yes," Jim nodded again. "He told me that if I wanted to get rid of the demons I would have to stop the drugs. Then he told me he would help me so I wouldn't have to do it on my own."

"That's all?"

"Well, after that I felt a lot of peace. The demons had gone completely, and I sort of fell asleep for a few moments. When I woke up, I wanted to talk to the man. Whoever he was, he had held me in place and talked to me. But he was gone. The manager didn't know where he'd gone."

"You mean the manager saw him, too?" Jennika asked.

"Yes, I guess everyone must have seen him. There were quite a few people standing around when all this was happening."

"And no one saw where he went?"

"No. But you want to know what's the weirdest thing of all?"

Jennika already felt funny about Jim's story, but she nodded.

"Well, I asked the manager what the man looked like who was bending over me, talking to me and holding my arms down. You know what he said? He told me the man had blond hair and was clean shaven. But that's not what I saw when I opened my eyes. I saw Jesus Christ. I mean it, Jennika. That's the only way I can describe him. He was talking to me very softly, and I knew he had come to warn me. If I don't change things now, with His help, the demons will get me. I believe that's why he appeared to me like that."

"But what about the blond guy? Was he talking to you or was some image in your hallucination?"

"I'm not sure. But everyone saw the man who held me down talking to me. They just couldn't hear what he said."

"So you think it was a warning?" Jennika asked tentatively. She had prayed that Jim's life would be drastically changed, but she had never expected this type of answer from the Lord.

"Yes. And I'm telling you now that I will never touch drugs again,

Jennika. I am going to turn to God and give Him a proper place in my life. I don't want his message to be in vain."

"Hmmm," Jennika said. "That's interesting."

"What?"

"Message. You were given a message from God. Do you know how messages from God were delivered in biblical times?"

Jim shook his head.

"From angels, Jim," she said slowly. "Maybe the man who was talking to you was an angel, telling you what the Lord wanted you to hear."

Jim thought a moment. "I don't know, Jen," he said after a while. "I guess we never will know who was really talking to me, who the messenger was. But I'm going to heed the message. I know that for sure."

Jim made several follow-up phone calls to the supermarket in search of the man who had helped him that afternoon. But the manager apparently never saw the man again. He had been available, helped in an emergency situation, and then disappeared. But not in vain.

Jim kept his word. For the next twenty years and still today, Jim Marlin has stayed away from all drugs and worked each year on making his marriage to Jennika better than ever. He has also maintained a dynamic relationship with God, one that began on a cold, supermarket floor in the grasp of a man who was, perhaps, an angel.

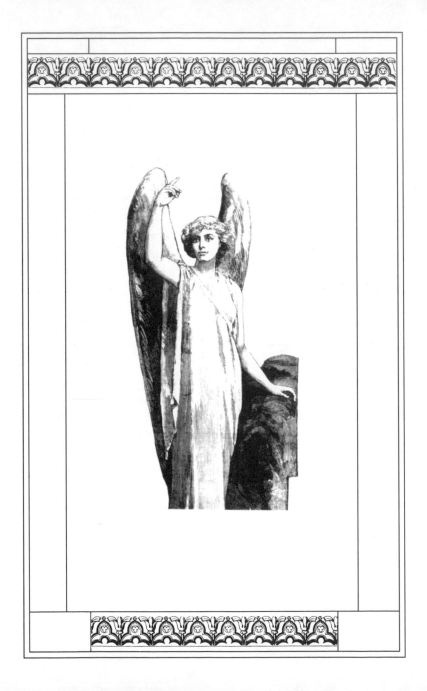

Angelic Reassurance

t was the summer of 1982, and Ann Holman and Linda Rust had been planning a trip for months. Their husbands and sons had been vacationing together at Lake Powell, boating and fishing for the past week. Now, on an early Saturday morning in Canoga Park, California, Ann and Linda were about to take their three small daughters and drive eight hours to Sedona, Arizona, where they would meet up with the men.

"Be sure to have the station wagon checked before you leave," Harley Rust had told his wife earlier that week. "You don't want to break down in the desert with those little girls."

Linda agreed. She took the wagon to a local mechanic's shop and had a complete tune-up done.

"Everything looks great, Mrs. Rust," the mechanic assured her. "Belts are fine, fluids are fine. Shouldn't have any trouble on the trip."

Linda thanked the man, and by Friday afternoon she and Ann were busy packing the wagon with things they would need for a long drive. Early Saturday morning, before the sun came up, the women and their children set out toward the desert on Interstate 10. They stopped in Indio for gasoline, and a local mechanic offered to check under the hood. After several minutes of intensely scrutinizing the engine, the mechanic straightened himself and shook his head in concern.

"Doesn't look good, ladies," he said ominously.

Linda moved closer to the car and stared at the engine. "What's wrong?"

"Fan belt's going," he said. "Might not snap for another hundred miles or so. Of course, if it snaps while you're driving, it could be dangerous."

Linda wrinkled her brow and motioned for Ann to join her. "He says the fan belt looks ready to snap and it could be dangerous," she told her friend and then turned back to the mechanic. "What could happen?" she asked.

"Well, not always, but sometimes the force will send it right through the hood and the windshield. Right into the passenger area."

Linda shuddered at the thought of the outcome if the fan belt flew into the area where the children were sitting. "What if we replaced it?" she asked.

"Of course, that would be the safest thing to do," he said slowly. "Cost about $300."

Linda was silent a moment, weighing the man's words. "We need to think it over," she said, dismissing the man and pulling Ann closer to her. "What do you think?"

"You just had the car checked," Ann said. "Don't you think your own mechanic would have told you if there'd been a problem with the fan belt?"

Linda nodded. "Maybe he's just trying to take us for $300. Here we are in the middle of nowhere, a couple of women and a bunch of little girls. What do we know?"

Ann pursed her lips and stared into the engine area. "I wish we knew more. I don't have any idea where the fan belt is or what it's supposed to look like."

"Me neither. What should we do?"

"Whatever you think. It's your car," Ann said, patting her friend on the back.

"OK. Let's pray for safety and drive on to Blythe. That's another two hours and we'll see what happens. We can get another opinion at a garage there."

Ann nodded, rounded up the girls, and strapped them into the car. Immediately she began praying, asking God for safety and discernment. If the belt was about to go, she prayed for a sign so that they would have the wisdom to pull over before anyone got hurt.

Prayer was nothing new for Ann and Linda. The women and their families had met while attending West Valley Christian Church in West Hills. Ann and Linda had learned to incorporate their faith into everything they did.

As Linda started the station wagon, she prayed aloud that God would guide them safely to Blythe and keep the car from breaking down until they were near a gas station. Even the little girls joined in the prayer.

"Please keep us safe, Jesus," seven-year-old Joy added from the backseat.

The next two hours passed slowly as the women remained silent, both continuing to pray as they drove. Despite their faith, there was tension in the air as they continued. When they were only a few miles from Blythe, the children needed to use a bathroom, and the women decided to turn off at a rest area a mile up the interstate. The stop was situated on a flat piece of desert land with an empty parking lot that circled a small hut in the center. Pulling into the deserted rest station, Linda parked the car and sent the girls toward the bathrooms. Then she lifted the hood of her wagon.

"Come here, Ann," she said. "Let's take a look at the engine. If it's getting worse, maybe we'll be able to see it now."

Ann joined her, and the women bent over and looked closely at the various engine parts, completely unaware of what they were looking at. Eventually they stood up, still staring at the engine and trying to distinguish one part from another and hoping to locate the fan belt. Suddenly they heard a voice.

"Can I help?"

The woman turned to see an unassuming Hispanic man standing directly behind them. He was dressed in jeans and a blue, button-down shirt, and he had dark hair and eyes. He smiled warmly, standing back a bit so as to not frighten the women. Still, they were startled at first, since they had not heard him walk up and did not see any other cars in the area. But the women were put at ease by something in the man's eyes, a gentleness they could not describe. Ann and Linda stepped aside, motioning for the man to take a look at the engine.

"A mechanic in Indio told us the fan belt was ready to snap," Linda explained. "But honestly we don't know what we're looking for."

The man smiled and moved closer to the car. For several minutes he looked at the engine, touching various parts and looking thoroughly at others. Finally, he stepped back and gazed directly into Linda's eyes, then Ann's.

"The car is fine," he said clearly and deliberately, much the way a parent would talk to children. "There are no mechanical problems at all. Relax and enjoy your trip."

The women nodded and moved once more toward the engine,

peering in at the parts, all of which still appeared foreign to them. At that moment they both realized how tense they had been for the past two hours. Although they had been praying constantly and believed that God would take care of them, they had not enjoyed the trip. Linda smiled and turned to thank the man for his reassurance.

But the man was gone.

"Hey, where'd he go?" Linda asked and Ann turned around. There was no one anywhere near them.

"That's impossible," Ann said softly. "Where could he have gone?"

The women stood planted in place scanning the grounds of the rest station. But the man in the blue shirt had disappeared.

For the next four hours the women drove on to Sedona without worrying about the car. Not until that evening did they discuss the man, his message, and his disappearance.

"After he told us everything was fine I just stopped worrying about it," Linda said.

Ann nodded. "Almost like he gave us a sense of peace, that there really wasn't anything wrong."

"Maybe God wanted us to know he had heard our prayers and we didn't need to be concerned about car trouble," Linda said, looking at her friend and speaking matter-of-factly. "There was no way he could have gone anywhere that quickly, Ann. You know who he was, don't you?"

"Do you really think so?"

Linda nodded and smiled.

"An angel?"

"Is there any other explanation?"

Ann shook her head slowly. "Amazing, isn't it?"

"Amazing grace."

Heavenly Help in the Emergency Room

t age eight, Joey Clark had been in hospital emergency rooms numerous times, but none of them as serious as that summer morning in 1990. Betty, the boy's mother, sat in the emergency room alone, praying quietly.

"I can't promise anything," the doctor had told her. "I'm sorry, Mrs. Clark. It doesn't look like he's going to make it this time."

Joey had joined the Clark family when he was only a few months old. At that time, Betty and Dan Clark were licensed foster parents for the state of California in Los Angeles County. Joey came to them on a clear, windy day one winter in 1982, a tiny baby with dark hair, big eyes, and a very still body.

"He has numerous physical and mental handicaps," the social worker had explained to Dan and Betty. "He may not live through the week. I know it won't be easy, but I need to know if you can take him. His mother is unable to care for him, and he needs a safe place to stay."

Betty swallowed hard, trying to keep from crying before the tiny handicapped child.

"We'll do our best," Dan spoke up, taking the baby gently in his arms. "He'll be our little son for as long as you need us to take care of him."

The Clarks had two daughters, both of whom were well into their teenaged years and busy with their own lives. Joey would take more time than the other foster children they'd taken in, but the Clarks had always relied on their faith in trying times, and usually grew stronger in the process. Dan figured this situation would be one of those occasions. He prayed silently for the child's health, and listened carefully as the social worker discussed detailed directions for caring for the special child in his arms.

Joey lived through the week as the Clarks developed a routine around the needy infant. Six months later, despite his handicaps, Joey seemed to be thriving. Betty checked with the social worker and found that the boy's mother did not feel capable of caring for a child with such severe handicaps.

"You shouldn't have him much longer," she added. "We're trying to place him in a home or a facility where he can be cared for full time."

Betty was shocked. "He doesn't need to be in a facility!" she said, outraged at the idea. "He is a child. He needs love and a family to care for him."

The social worker sighed. "Yes, I know that, Mrs. Clark. But Joey's disabilities are so severe, he will need special care all his life. He will never speak or walk or even be able to feed himself."

"But he's a child, still," Betty responded. "He needs love more than he needs special care. Especially from an institute. We'll keep him here until you find a home for him."

The social worker agreed, but six months later she had still not found a permanent home for the little boy. Dan and Betty and their daughters celebrated the boy's first birthday and a few days later realized that the social worker was right. A home might never be found for the child they'd come to love as their own.

"I guess we have just one choice," Dan said one evening.

"The home is right here, isn't it?" Betty asked, tears filling her eyes as she smiled, knowing her husband felt the same way.

Dan nodded. "Let's look into it."

Over the next few months, the Clarks went through the necessary steps to take legal custody of the boy. In order to receive state financial assistance for Joey's medical needs, they could not adopt him. But he would now be their legal dependent, and in their eyes, he would be their son. When the procedure was final, the Clarks threw another birthday party for Joey and were thrilled to see his eyes show signs of responding.

Years passed and Joey continued to show delight in the attention he received. Although he was not born with the physical ability to sit, stand, or speak, Joey could make sounds and use his eyes to show emotion. When Joey was still very young, the Clarks were able to distinguish between Joey's expressions and knew when he was hungry, tired, or in need of extra attention. He would always need to be hand-fed through tubing, and he would never develop the independence of caring for himself. But the Clarks loved him with a fierce, protective love that brought deep meaning to their lives. Never did they regret adopting the boy or give any thought to the time and energy Joey required of them.

"I know he can't do the things another little boy might be able to do," Dan would say when people asked about Joey. "But he has his own accomplishments. And for how much he tries, I couldn't be prouder of him. I love him so much. More, probably, than I could have loved a child without his problems."

Illness was a part of Joey's life, a part that worried his parents often. Because he had so little control over his muscle function, Joey did not cough the way an able-bodied child would. For that reason, he often contracted respiratory infections, and several times in his young life he had been hospitalized for pneumonia and other life-threatening problems.

That was the case in the summer of 1990, when Joey had been hospitalized for pneumonia and released. But now, despite antibiotics, Joey had gotten much worse and he wasn't eating. Finally, in the hours after midnight, Betty was awakened by the sound of Joey gasping for air. She raced him to the nearest emergency room but by then her son was barely breathing. Doctors had tried to put a tube in the boy's stomach to force feed him but they had not inserted it correctly and now in addition to his infection he had food spilling into the cavity of his upper torso. His chances of surviving emergency surgery in his condition were very slim.

After the doctor's ominous diagnosis, Betty knew she had just one way to find peace. She found a quiet corner in the waiting room— which at 3 a.m. was completely empty—hung her head and began to pray.

"Lord," she prayed in a whispered voice. "Please help my little boy. I love him so, and I know he's scared right now. Please help him to breathe."

At that instant, Betty heard someone enter the room through the open door. She looked up and saw a small man dressed in janitorial clothing and pulling a mop and water bucket on wheels. Something about the man's face seemed unnaturally kind and Betty stared at him curiously. His uniform was rumpled, and he seemed almost stooped in the humble demeanor of servant.

"I have something to tell you," the man said softly, looking directly at Betty. "A message from God."

Betty was taken aback by the man's statement. But she leaned forward so she could hear him better, never once feeling afraid of him. She waited as the man took one step closer and smiled gently.

"He's going to be OK," the man said. *"Malachi 4:2."*

Then, before Betty could ask him any of the dozens of questions that raced through her mind, the man turned around and left.

Betty stood up quickly and moved across the room toward the door. She stepped into the hallway expecting to see the man a few feet away, but he was gone. None of the other doors in the hallway were open. Betty couldn't imagine how he could have gotten away so quickly, especially pulling a bucket of water.

She waited a moment, looking up and down the hallway in both directions, hoping to see which way the man had gone. But after a while she turned around and moved slowly back to her seat. How had the man known about Joey? Could he possibly have known that she was waiting for news about whether her son would live through the night? And what did the Bible verse he had mentioned have to do with her situation. Donna was baffled as she considered the man's words.

Finally, she resolved to find the man and learn why he had told her everything was going to be all right and who had told him to tell her. She went up to the emergency check-in counter.

"I need to speak with one of your hospital janitors," she said matter-of-factly. "He was small, about this tall," she used her hand to show how high the man had stood. "And he stopped by the waiting room here a few minutes ago. I'm not sure where he is right now, but I need to talk to him. Could you page him?"

The receptionist pulled out a schedule and scanned it slowly.

"That's what I thought," she said, her voice puzzled.

"What?"

"The janitors," she said, looking up from the paper and staring at Betty. "They've all gone home. They left three hours ago."

Betty shook her head. "No, there must be someone else, another janitor or something. The one I talked to walked right into that room," she pointed toward the waiting area. "I just saw him not ten minutes ago. He's somewhere down that hallway."

"Well, all I can tell you, ma'am, is he doesn't work at this hospital. Our janitors went home. They're all off the clock. Besides, I don't think we even have a janitor that fits the description you gave me."

Betty stepped backward and turned around, moving slowly toward the sofa in the waiting room. She was still trying to understand who the man might have been, when Joey's doctor walked into the room.

"Well, Mrs. Clark. I have to say it's nothing short of a miracle," the doctor said, breaking into a smile. "Joey wasn't breathing well at all. In fact, ten minutes ago we thought we were losing him. Then he suddenly began coughing and in a few minutes he was breathing normally again. I can't explain it."

"He's OK, then?" Betty asked, fresh tears filling her eyes as she rose to meet the doctor.

"He's still sick, but the danger's passed."

Joey went home two days later, but Betty never forgot how close she and Dan came to losing their son that morning. The Bible verse, *Malachi 4:2*, talked about revering God's name so that healing would come. She always kept the verse with her after that and found herself reciting it numerous times as she and Joey faced the trials that came with his condition. But no matter how sick Joey became, she never forgot the small man in the janitorial uniform who delivered what she knows was an angelic message of hope.

"God used that man, whoever he was, to reassure me that Joey was going to be all right. My prayers had been heard."

The Vanishing Prison Guard

ohn Mark was handsome and carefree, twenty-five years old and at a crossroads. Raised in a God-fearing home, he knew he had strayed away from his upbringing. But recently he had begun to experiment with drugs and a faster lifestyle, which threatened to destroy his chances to ever turn back. He was in college, but without any particular direction in life. He sometimes wondered what point there was in working so hard for an uncertain future.

These were his thoughts one night in 1982 as he drove along the Florida Turnpike. Why not, he told himself, give in to the pressures around him? At least the parties he'd been attending—and the drugs he'd been doing—gave him some satisfaction. Even if it was temporary.

The longer Mark thought about his situation, the more he began to believe that he should drop out of college. Life would be simpler, something seemed to be telling him, if he weren't so burdened with responsibilities.

"And the last thing I need to get messed up with right now is church," he mumbled out loud, peering straight ahead into the dark Florida night. That had been his mother's suggestion but he had rebelled against the idea since first hearing it. "Never helped me any before," he'd told her. "Can't help me much now."

Mark drove on until, suddenly, he spotted what looked like a fully dressed prison guard hitchhiking along the side of the road. Mark had never picked up a hitchhiker, but something about the man suggested he was on the way to work and genuinely in need of a ride. Mark pulled over and rolled down his window. The man stooped down and looked inside, smiling.

"Need a ride?" Mark asked tentatively.

"Thanks, I was hoping you'd stop," he said, each word carefully measured. "Car's broken down."

Mark nodded in understanding and opened his car door. He hadn't seen any broken-down cars alongside the roadway, but the man seemed kind enough. Mark was not afraid that his hitchhiking might be some kind of ruse to rob or harm him.

Mark glanced at his passenger and saw that the man was well into his fifties, with graying hair and a moustache. He had kind, blue eyes and a face that seemed filled with light. His prison guard uniform was perfectly pressed, and he seemed strangely out of place in it.

"You a prison guard?" Mark asked, picking up speed and resuming his drive along the highway.

The man nodded. "Just got off work. State penitentiary back down the road a ways." There was only one such prison in the vicinity and Mark knew the place.

"What's your name?"

"Kenneth. Kenneth Hawes. Worked at the prison for the past ten years."

Mark was silent a moment. "I have a long drive ahead of me. Where are you going?" Mark noticed that the man seemed unusually calm and relaxed, considering he was with a stranger in an unfamiliar car after a breakdown of his own.

"Home," he said softly, smiling at Mark as if home were the most wonderful place in the world. "About an hour up the road. Now, why don't you tell me what's on your mind?"

Mark was unsure what to make of the man, but he shrugged and started telling him his age and what he was studying in school.

"No," the man said softly. "Tell me about the crossroad."

Mark stared at the man, wondering how he could have known to ask such a question.

"What?" he asked.

"You know what I mean. You have some choices you're trying to make, don't you?"

Mark felt strangely uncomfortable, as if the man could somehow read his thoughts. But he shrugged once again, convincing himself that the man could not possibly have known anything about his personal life. The stranger was only lonely and looking for conversation.

"Yeah, I know what you mean," he said. With a loud sigh, Mark decided to tell the man the truth. He told him about his upbringing and how his parents prayed for him daily.

"But I'm different now, that kind of life is in my past," Mark said, waving his hand as if to indicate he would never again involve himself in organized religion.

"No," the man's voice was sudden and firm. Mark looked at him; he was shaking his head. "It's closer than you think."

"You're a prison guard, what would you know?" Mark asked, suddenly irritated with this strange man's intrusive comments.

"I do know," he said. The man's answer was not defensive or

angry, but he spoke with a finality that set Mark on edge.

"Well, that's about it. I have a couple ways I could go and it looks like I'm taking the one that fits me best. Forget school, forget religion. Forget everything."

The man said nothing. He stared straight ahead for several minutes before turning again toward Mark. "Mark, you know there's only one way, don't you?"

"Look, thanks for listening but I'm tired of talking. My exit is coming up. Where can I drop you off?"

The man smiled, his attitude unchanged by Mark's brusqueness. With a series of directions, he led Mark to a busy intersection. "This is close enough, Mark."

"Listen, I can take you to your house. Really. It's too late to be walking home alone out here."

"I can find my home from here," he said, shaking his head firmly and turning to face Mark squarely. "Make the right choice, son. Now. You still have the chance, you know."

He climbed out, shut the door and waved once before turning away and walking up the street. For a moment Mark wanted to follow him, to spend more time talking with him and to glean something from the wisdom he seemed to possess. But the night was late and he had school in the morning. He pulled his car back onto the main road and headed back toward the turnpike.

Through the night and into the next morning Mark thought over everything the man had said. How had he known so much? And why would he have been hitch-hiking home when he lived so far from the prison? Finally Mark decided he needed to talk to the man once more. He called the prison from his dormitory that afternoon.

"I'd like to speak to Kenneth Hawes," Mark said. "He's a prison guard."

There was a pause on the other end. "I don't believe he works here."

Mark furrowed his eyebrows. "Of course he works there. He was working yesterday evening, and I gave him a ride home. He had his uniform on and everything."

"Well, sir, I can let you talk with my supervisor, but to my knowledge there isn't any prison guard named Kenneth Hawes at this facility."

"Fine," Mark said, and he could feel his frustration rising. "Let me talk to your supervisor."

The supervisor spent ten minutes convincing Mark that there wasn't now and never had been a Kenneth Hawes employed at the prison. At Mark's request, she also checked the other prison facilities in the state but none of them employed a Kenneth Hawes either.

Stunned, Mark hung up the phone. The man had ridden with him for more than an hour, giving him advice about his life and trying to point him in the right direction. Now he had disappeared, almost as if he had never existed.

Frustrated and wanting to share the story, Mark called his mother that evening and told her what had happened.

"Sometimes God gets our attention in interesting ways," his mother said quietly. "Did you ever think that he might have been an angel?"

"An angel? Like in the Bible stories?" Mark asked doubtfully.

"Why not? God is still God, and His ways aren't so different now than in Bible times," she said.

For several weeks Mark considered the possibility until, finally, he was convinced that his mother was right. Kenneth must have been an angel sent to guide him through a time in his life when he had crucial choices to make. How better for God to get his attention than with a prison guard, especially in light of the choices he'd been making lately.

Almost overnight, Mark decided he would no longer involve himself in harmful activities, such as drugs and all-night parties. Instead, over the next year he doubled his efforts toward school and began attending church again. In the process, he found a peace and assurance he had never believed could exist. Eventually, Mark earned a degree in telecommunications and went on to serve as a news reporter for one of the television news shows in southern Florida.

More than a decade later, he is as certain as ever that God used an angel to change his life.

Heavenly
Visitor

ussell Johnson's third heart attack happened on the job. As captain of the Wayne, Michigan, fire department, Russell didn't need to don a uniform and fight fires any more, especially after his two recent heart attacks. But on a warm day in 1974, Russell couldn't resist. He was in the heat of battling a raging fire when the pain struck.

"Help!" he shouted as loudly as he could above the roar of the fire.

One of the firefighters nearby heard him and summoned help. Together they carried him out of the burning building, and paramedics rushed him to the hospital. When the danger had passed, Russell took the only choice the doctors were giving him if he wanted to live. He retired.

Having raised four daughters, Russell and his wife, Jean, decided to move to Punta Gorda, Florida, where they bought a small home and began living the life of retirees. Although they had very little money, they found enjoyment in the regular visits they received from their four daughters and their families. Russell also set up a workshop in his garage, where he spent hours repairing church organs and making dollhouses.

One afternoon in November 1985, Russell, now sixty-five years old, was tinkering out in his workshop, making tiny shingles for a dollhouse he was building, when there was a knock on the front door. Moments later Jean entered the shop, her face ghostly white.

"There's a huge man at the door," she said, her voice barely more than a whisper. "He's dressed in rags and I don't know what to do. He's waiting there."

Russell set down his tools on the workbench and led the way back into the house. From the peephole in the front door, Russell could see his wife was right. The man was possibly six feet five inches and easily weighed 275 pounds. He was a mountain of a man, dirty, and wearing torn clothes. He carried a small satchel. Russell opened the door and smiled.

"Can I help you, sir?"

The man lowered his eyes humbly and cleared his throat. "Yes, I was wondering if you might have some work I could do in exchange for some food."

Russell was struck by the man's gentle personality. As he and Jean stood looking at the man filling their doorway, they were suddenly no longer afraid of the man.

"Well," Russell said slowly. "I haven't got any work for you. But we can sure get you something to eat."

The man looked up, and his eyes seemed to glimmer with a new sense of hope. Jean turned and headed toward the kitchen.

"I don't know how I can thank you kind people," he said. "See, I'm from Texas, got caught up in the oil crunch and thought I could find work if I headed out here."

Russell nodded his understanding. "You look pretty tired," he said. "Can I get you something to rest on?"

"Yes, in fact I am pretty tired. Been walking much of the day. I'd appreciate a chair."

Russell went out back and brought back three folding chairs. He set them up on the driveway and joined the man outside. The large man seemed very tired and thankful for the place to sit. For several minutes, the men sat together in a comfortable silence.

As Russell watched the stranger, he wondered what terrible twists the man's life had taken to bring him to the place of begging for food. He and Jean had never known a time where there wasn't food on the table or a roof over their heads. But in recent years, their finances had become very tight; he could only imagine how terrible it would be to have no home and no idea where one's next meal was coming from.

The day before, Russell remembered, he and his wife had taken a trip to the market and carefully bought food for the week, spending all the money they had until their next pension check later that month.

Russell was certain that Jean understood the hasty way he had agreed to feed the man. Even though they had precious little, they had more than this poor man. Russell was suddenly overwhelmed with thankfulness. The good Lord had always provided them with all they needed. Now he was glad to help this stranger, even if it was only by providing the man with a meal.

Jean finished making a plate of sandwiches and brought it outside with a pitcher of iced tea. The man thanked her and then hungrily began eating. He finished four sandwiches and several large glasses of iced tea before wiping his mouth and standing to leave.

"That was perfect," he said. "You don't know how thankful I am."

"Let me go back in the house and pack you a dinner," Jean said, turning and heading toward the front door. Russell smiled. He and

Jean thought alike. He had been about to suggest the same thing. Russell turned back toward the man.

"Sir, have you got any money on you?" Russell asked curiously.

"Why, yes, I have thirteen cents," the man answered, his voice ringing with honesty.

"Stay right here," Russell said. "I'll be right back."

Russell went into the house and found a dollar in his billfold. Then he began scrounging through the family sugar bowl which always contained loose change. He managed to find five dollars, which he carefully carried outside. Jean had already joined the man by then and was handing him a sack dinner. She described the bag's contents and apologized that she couldn't provide him with anymore for the next day. Russell stepped forward.

"Here." Russell held the money out to the man. "Maybe this will help you get through another day or so a little bit easier."

The man took the money and placed it carefully in his satchel. Then he looked up at Russell and Jean.

"You people have been so kind to me," he said, his eyes moist. "Thank you." He paused a moment as if searching for something else to say. "Thank you."

He turned away, walking toward the sidewalk. When he reached the bottom of their driveway, he turned to face them and raised his hand in what appeared to be almost a salute.

"God bless you!" he said, his voice filled with emotion. "And thank you."

Then he turned and walked the length of the Johnson's corner house and turned right, heading along the side of their house and backyard toward the freeway, a few blocks away.

The Johnsons headed back into the house, shaken by the man's thankfulness. It had felt wonderful to help someone who was far needier than they had ever been. Indeed, as their preacher had often said, there had been a true blessing in giving. As he walked into the house, Russell immediately made his way into the backyard to resume work in his workshop. As he did, he leaned over the fence to say a final goodbye to the man, who by then should have been passing along the side of their backyard.

But the man had disappeared.

There were no bushes or trees or places to hide. Russell calculated the time he had taken to walk from the front yard into the back. Seven seconds or less, he figured. They had seen the man walking along the sidewalk that bordered the right side of their property. He was heading toward the freeway, which meant he would have to walk along the edge of their backyard and beyond. Yet somehow, in only a few seconds, the man had disappeared. Russell stood rooted in place. How could the man have disappeared like that?

"Jean," he called. "Come here."

Jean walked outside. "What is it?"

"That man, wasn't he walking this way?"

"Yes." Jean pointed toward their side fence. "If you look, you should be able to see him walking toward the freeway."

Russell shook his head. "He's gone, Jean. Nowhere."

Jean furrowed her eyebrows and joined her husband next to their fence. He was right. The man had disappeared. For the next fifteen minutes, Jean and Russell scoured the sidewalks that ran in front of and beside their corner house. Finally, they asked Joe, who lived across the street. Russell liked to say that Joe knew how many sparrows came and went through the neighborhood on a given day. Certainly he would know which way the man had gone.

The Johnsons found Joe sitting in his outdoor rocker sipping lemonade, which was how Joe typically spent his afternoons and early evenings. Russell described the large man who had visited their home and his haggard appearance.

"Haven't seen him at all," Joe said. "You sure he was by your place today?"

"Of course we're sure," Russell said, pointing across the street at his own driveway. "The wife fixed him a bunch of sandwiches. Sat right out there and ate 'em."

"That's strange," Joe said. "I've been home all day. Didn't see anyone over at your house. Guess I can't help you."

Discouraged at what had become of the man and what his fate might be with so little food and money, Russell and Jean decided to head back into their home. For several minutes, the two sat in their living room in silence, each wondering about the man who had shared lunch with them and how he had disappeared so quickly.

"Something special about the man, don't you think, Russell?" Jean asked softly.

"Something very special. Guess we'll never know who he was or what might become of him. I just wish there had been something else we might have done."

Jean paused a moment. "What if he was an angel?"

Russell chuckled lightly. "Come on, you're not serious are you? Angels don't dress like that."

"Yes," Jean insisted. "You remember the Bible verse about being careful to entertain strangers, for by doing so, some have entertained angels without knowing it? Well, what if he was that kind of stranger?"

Russell thought for a moment. He and Jean had not been regular church attenders in recent years, but they still considered themselves strong believers.

"I guess it sounds familiar," Russell said slowly. "So, you think this was some kind of test or something?"

"I don't know," Jean said, smiling and taking her husband's hand. "I keep thinking of that scripture that says, 'Whatsoever you do for the least of these, you do unto Me.' Maybe that's why we feel so good about what happened and the small way in which we could help."

Jean was silent a moment and then continued. "Maybe the man wasn't an angel, maybe he was just a guy who was down on his luck," she said. "But I can't explain where the man went and neither can you."

After that, the Johnsons told no one about the strange man, his humble gratefulness and his sudden disappearance. But one month later, Jean was opening Christmas cards, when she grew suddenly and strangely silent.

"Russell," she said loudly, clearly distracted by the card she was holding. "Someone must be playing a practical joke on you."

Russell entered the kitchen. "What is it?" he asked, walking up to where she sat at the dining room table.

"This card," she held a simple Christmas card up for her husband to see. "It's signed, 'love from, your Christian friend.' There's no return address."

"Let's see that," Russell said, taking the card.

"That's not all of it," she said, holding up a slip of paper. "This was inside."

Russell took the paper and stared at it. It was a cashier's check made out to the Johnsons for $500.

"Jean, this is no joke, this is a real legal-like check," Russell said, his eyes wide. "Who could have done such a thing?"

Jean shook her head, speechless. She was unable to imagine which of their friends might have been able to spare such a large amount of money. But it wasn't until the next year at Christmas time, when the Johnsons received a similar card with another cashier's check for $500 that they were struck by an idea.

"Do you think there could be some connection," Jean asked her husband that year, "between these cards and that man we helped?"

"I don't think we'll ever know. But I still say it felt better helping him out that day than it feels to get this money in the mail. Even though we certainly could use it."

For the next three years the Johnsons received a Christmas card from their mysterious Christian friend, accompanied by a $500 cashier's check. After that, the mysterious cards stopped coming. Only then did they share the story with their children.

"We were afraid they'd think we were crazy," says Russell, who saved each of the Christmas cards, the envelopes they came in, and copies of the cashier's checks. "This is one of those stories that seems hard to believe. But it's true. Every word."

Even now, Russell and Jean are not convinced the anonymous cards and cashier's checks are related to their helping a hungry stranger—and maybe even an angel—weeks before Christmas.

"We never had any thought of getting something back," Russell says. "That isn't what giving is all about."

The Boy and the Bus

here were times when Dr. Mike Barns wondered why he went into the medical profession. People were always complaining about one ailment or another, and none of them understood that he was a busy man. Very busy. The way his schedule had been for the past several years, he wondered how he had survived. There had been a time, long ago, when he had been involved in his church, active in his faith. But prayer and devotions took time—a precious commodity Dr. Barns no longer had. And so he had let those things that had once brought him such peace and joy pass from his life almost completely. By the world's standards, Dr. Barns, at twenty-nine years old, had everything anyone could ever want. Good looks, youth, more than enough money, and a successful career that placed him in a position of esteem among his peers.

He gave little thought to much of this as he raced his BMW across a two-lane Arizona desert highway toward Lake Tahoe, situated along the border between

Nevada and California. The vacation would last less than a week, but for months Dr. Barns had been looking forward to getting away from his overwhelming responsibilities. He stared straight ahead, trying only to clear his mind and his body of the hectic pace it had become accustomed to.

Picking up his cellular telephone, he tried to make a call. An hour had passed since he'd checked in with his office exchange. Duty and a tendency to perfectionism, rather than love for his patients, drove him to worry constantly about the messages he was missing. He dialed the number but nothing happened. Angrily, he tapped the receiver on the steering wheel.

"Come on," he said, his teeth clenched.

He dialed again but still nothing happened. "Stupid machine," he muttered, glancing at the vast expanse of desert that surrounded him. "Supposed to work anywhere."

He glanced down at his speedometer and noticed he was driving twenty miles over the speed limit.

"Just can't slow down, can you, Barns?" he said aloud, laughing bitterly and forcing himself to slow his pace and savor the solitude of the drive.

At that moment he saw a small figure ahead, on the side of the highway. Barns took his foot off the gas pedal and coasted, scanning the highway ahead and behind him for a broken-down car. There was none. He was getting closer to the figure, and he realized it was a small boy, dressed in scouting gear and wearing a red baseball cap. The boy was waving at him frantically, motioning for him to stop.

"Oh, brother," Barns sighed, swerving off the road and coming to a sudden stop. He rolled down his tinted window. "What do you need, boy?" he asked impatiently.

"Sir, I need a ride. Right away. Please . . ." The boy's voice was filled with anxiety, and Barns wondered if he was going to cry.

Barns paused a moment, considering his schedule and his plan to avoid all contact with people until the week's end. He sighed audibly. "All right," he said, opening the passenger door of his BMW. "Get in."

Appearing very upset, the boy nodded quickly and climbed into the car. "Straight ahead," he said urgently.

After a few moments of silence, the boy spoke again. "There, up ahead, turn right," he said.

"That's a dirt road," Barns said, frustrated by the boy. "Do you know what all that dust will do to my car, huh?" he asked.

The boy shook his head. "Please take it, sir. It leads to a paved road, I promise," he said quickly.

Barns followed the boy's directions, taking the dirt road until it turned into a paved road which began to wind up a mountainside.

"How far up?" Barns asked, glancing at the boy and wondering when he would find time to have his car washed again. Just as he had predicted moments earlier, the dirt road had covered the shiny black paint with a fine layer of light brown silt.

The boy pointed up the road. "Take this a few more miles to the top," he said.

Barns sighed aloud and drove in silence toward the mountaintop. As they approached it, Barns began to hear the faint sound of high-pitched screams. He was suddenly confused. "Where are we going?" he asked, looking strangely at the boy.

"To help," the boy said. "Hurry."

Barns drove a bit faster, something in his cold heart warmed slightly by the boy's attitude and a growing concern over the screaming sounds, which were growing louder by the minute. The boy held up his hand. "Stop here," he said. Then he pointed over to the edge of the road, which had no guard rail and led to a sharp drop-off, hundreds of feet down into a canyon.

Barns climbed out of his car and heard the sound clearly now. It was children, dozens of them screaming for help. Instantly, he ran toward the edge of the road and looked down. What he saw horrified him. There was a yellow school bus perched precariously on its side and resting on a ledge of rocks at least two hundred feet down the canyon. Barns turned around and ran back to his car with the little boy running alongside him.

Forgetting that it hadn't worked only thirty minutes earlier, Barns picked up his cellular telephone and dialed the number for emergency service. It worked instantly.

"Quick, send ambulances and paramedics," he said quickly. "A bus has flipped over the canyon and it's filled with children. I'm a doctor. I'll do my best until you get here."

Barns gave the dispatch operator specific directions to the site and then hung up the phone. He placed both hands on the shoulders of the little boy beside him and looked intently into his eyes. "Stay here," he said. "I'm going down the hill to help out."

The boy nodded and watched as Barns ran toward the road's edge and then disappear over the side. The canyon was incredibly steep, but Barns was able to use rocks and vegetation to help make his way to the disabled bus. Children were reaching out the windows, screaming for help, and smoke was beginning to fill the cabin area.

"Lord, help me on this one," he prayed silently. And then he got to work.

He made his way carefully to the front of the bus, but the hydraulic doors were pinned shut against a jagged rock. He began to kick and push the rock until finally it fell away, tumbling violently down the steep canyon. Barns watched it fall and realized the rescue would have to be slow and cautious if he was to get any of the children up the hillside. One wrong move and he and the children would certainly fall to their deaths.

Just then, he heard the distant sound of sirens, and he was instantly thankful. He could begin helping the children out of the bus, but the effort would take several strong adults if it were to be successful. Barns was still trying to open the bus's doors when emergency personnel began filing cautiously down the hill.

"Everyone all right?" one of the paramedics yelled.

"Not sure," Barns responded. "They're real upset, and it's starting to fill up with smoke. We have to hurry."

"You the doctor who made the call?" the man asked, joining Barns at the bus's door.

"Yes."

"A fall like this one means lots of possible neck injuries, back injuries, that kind of thing," the paramedic said as others joined them, forming a human chain and carrying a thick cable from the road's edge to where the bus lay. Each child would be placed into a carrier, which would, in turn, be attached to the cable to prevent any of them from falling into the canyon.

"Let's hurry," the paramedic said.

Barns nodded. "We need to move carefully. The ground isn't very stable."

Ambulances were still arriving as Barns and the paramedic finally opened the bus doors and gently lifted out the nearest child. Barns did an initial check and deemed that the little girl miraculously had no neck or back injuries. The child was placed in a basket and handed from one paramedic to the next until she was safely at the top of the hill. There she was placed into an ambulance where paramedics immediately began checking the extent of her injuries.

Working together, Barns and the paramedics were able to take each of the twenty-five children from the bus and get them safely to the top of the hill. As time passed, Barns completely forgot about the little boy up on the road who was supposed to be waiting for him in his BMW. He was completely absorbed in the work at hand.

When it appeared that their efforts were finished, one of the paramedics climbed into the bus for a final look. Barns and the others watched from nearby, waiting for the signal that the bus was empty. Instead, the paramedic climbed out and shook his head, his face grim from what he'd just seen.

"One more," he shouted. "I'll need some help."

"How badly is he hurt?" Barns asked, moving toward the bus.

The paramedic shook his head, looking down at the ground. "He didn't make it," he said. "Just didn't make it."

Barns nodded, feeling the sting of tears in his eyes. As a doctor, he had never completely understood the gift he had of helping people overcome illness and injury until now. For the past hour, rescuing one crying child after another, Barns's heart had changed completely. He felt only a great sense of loss now that one of the children hadn't made it.

He moved carefully toward the bus. "I'll help," he said. Once inside, he followed closely behind the paramedic, climbing over the sides of one seat after another as they made their way to the back of the bus.

"He's over there," the paramedic said, pointing to a small corner near the bus's emergency door, which was pinned against the wall of the canyon.

"Looks like a broken neck," the paramedic said softly.

Barns moved into place and got a look at the limp body of the little boy who had been killed in the accident.

"No," he said. "It can't be." His voice was a haunting whisper as he rested back on his heels. His face grew startlingly pale as the paramedic stared at him strangely. After all, the man was a doctor and the paramedic did not expect him to react so strongly to the sight of a child's body. He had certainly seen death before.

"Are you OK?" the paramedic asked. "I can get someone else if this is too hard for you."

Barns shook his head violently. "It's *impossible*," he said, and the paramedic wondered if he were perhaps in shock because of the trauma of the lengthy rescue. "It's him."

"Do you know this boy?" the paramedic asked as he turned to look at the child.

"The little boy who brought me here," Barns said.

The paramedic wrinkled his brow in confusion. "I think you need some fresh air, Doc," he said. But Barns shook his head.

"I'm fine," he said. "Come on, let's get to work."

Barns knew it was impossible. But the still little body before him was the same boy who had been standing on the highway, the same boy who had given him directions up the hillside. He wore a scouting uniform and a red baseball cap. Barns was certain he was the same boy.

The paramedic watched Barns's reaction curiously and shrugged. "OK. We need to get him up the hill."

The men worked together to move the boy's body out of the bus and up the hill. As they worked, Barns wondered if he might have been mistaken. Perhaps the boys were twin brothers. There had to be an explanation. As they reached the road, Barns set the boy's body down and hurried across the road to his car. He had told the boy to stay in the car until he was finished. But as he approached it and opened the car door, he could see that the boy was gone.

"Hey," he yelled, running toward the fire captain who had overseen the entire operation from the road. "A little boy showed me where this accident was. I told him to wait for me in the car over there. Blond hair, blue eyes, red baseball cap, wearing a scouting uniform. Did you see where he went?"

The captain shook his head curiously. "Hasn't been anyone up here but us," he said. "When we got here, we checked that car, looking for whoever made the call. It was empty. Wasn't anyone up here at all."

Barns was incredulous. He moved away to a private spot on the road where he would be alone. He sat on the roadway and dropped his head into his hands. He replayed the incidents of the past two hours in his mind. The boy had definitely been real. He had waved him down and guided him toward the bus. Barns knew he never would have found the accident site if it hadn't been for the boy and his patient insistence that they drive to the top of the mountain.

Suddenly, Barns began to think the situation through. Until now he hadn't considered some of the obviously strange details surrounding the boy's appearance on the side of the highway. How had the boy walked more than five miles down the mountainside and out toward the highway by himself? If he had been in the bus, how had he escaped without any help? And how had he suddenly disappeared in the moments after Barns had made the emergency call? Most of all, who could explain the tiny covered body they'd brought up the hill? He looked identical to the child who had led him to the accident scene.

At that instant, chills ran the length of Dr. Barns's spine. When they passed, he was engulfed in a feeling of peace and a sudden understanding. Was it possible? Could the boy have been an angel, taking the image of the small little boy who had died in the accident? Barns closed his eyes and began crying. Perhaps God had hoped to teach him some kind of lesson here. Indeed, Barns knew with everything in him that he would never again be the same calloused man he had become. A person's life was so tenuous, so brief. But Barns knew he had been unable to see the value of the people behind his patients.

"Never again," Barns cried quietly, shaking his head in disgust at his former blindness. "Thank you, God. Whatever happened here, whoever that little boy was, thank you."

"You OK?" one of the paramedics asked as he approached him.

Barns nodded, wiping the tears from his face and standing up. "I need to see that boy once more," he said, moving past the paramedic toward the covered body several feet away. Gently he removed the tarp from his face, feeling the now familiar wave of shock. There was no doubt. He was the same boy. Barns bent down and softly brushed a lock of the child's blond hair back under his baseball cap.

"Goodbye little boy," he whispered, fresh tears flooding his eyes. "Whoever you are, I thank you."

Have You Had
an Angel Encounter?

If you would like to share a story involving an angel encounter—an unusual incident involving someone who seemed to be a real person until they disappeared or with someone who after further research never really existed—I would very much appreciate hearing from you. Your story may be used in an upcoming volume of angel encounters.

Please write a brief account of your experience, and include your name, address, telephone number, and other pertinent details of the encounter. If you would rather have your real name left out of the story, should it appear in print, please mention this in your letter. The author cannot guarantee that your story will be published, but your effort will be much appreciated all the same.

Address your angel encounters to:
Kelsey Tyler
P.O. Box 264
Clarkdale, Arizona 86324-9998